OLD THINGS AND NEW:

A STRATEGY FOR EDUCATION

Frederick E. Crowe, S.J.

OLD THINGS AND NEW:

A STRATEGY FOR EDUCATION

Supplementary Issue of the Lonergan Workshop journal

Volume 5

Fred Lawrence, Editor

Scholars Press
Atlanta, Georgia

OLD THINGS AND NEW:

A STRATEGY FOR EDUCATION

©1985

Frederick E. Crowe, S.J.

Library of Congress Cataloging-in-Publication Data

Crowe, Frederick E.
  Old things and new.

  Supplementary issue of Lonergan workshop, v.5,
  Bibliography: p.
  1. Education--Philosophy. 2. Teaching. 3. Education, Higher.
4. Education--Religious · aspects--Christianity. 5. Lonergan,
Bernard J.F. I. Lonergan workshop. V. 5 (Supplement)
II. Title.
LB1025.2.C675   1985   370'.1   85-18327
ISBN 0-89130-869-5

BT
738.17
.C76
1985

Printed in the United States of America
on acid-free paper

JESUIT - KRAUSS - McCORMICK - LIBRARY
1100 EAST 55th STREET
CHICAGO, ILLINOIS 60615

CONTENTS

BIBLIOGRAPHICAL NOTE

There is frequent reference in this book to various works of Bernard Lonergan. Here are publication data on those most often referred to.

Collection: Papers by Bernard Lonergan, S.J. Edited by Frederick E. Crowe, S.J. New York: Herder and Herder, and London: Darton, Longman & Todd, 1967. Now out of print.

Insight: A Study of Human Understanding. Originally published, London: Longmans, Green and Co., and New York: Philosophical Library, Inc., 1957. Now available in paperback (fourth edition), San Francisco: Harper & Row.

Method in Theology. London: Darton, Longman & Todd, 1972. Published in the United States, originally by Herder and Herder, more recently by The Seabury Press. The American stock now being exhausted, a reissue through another publisher is in preparation.

A Second Collection: Papers by Bernard J. F. Lonergan, S.J. Edited by William F. J. Ryan, S.J., and Bernard J. Tyrrell, S.J. London: Darton, Longman & Todd, and Philadelphia: The Westminster Press, 1974.

A Third Collection: Papers by Bernard J. F. Lonergan, S.J. Edited by Frederick E. Crowe, S.J. Mahwah, NJ: Paulist Press, and London: Geoffrey Chapman, 1985.

Verbum: Word and Idea in Aquinas. Edited by David B. Burrell, C.S.C. Notre Dame, IN: University of Notre Dame Press, and London: Darton, Longman & Todd, 1967.

Articles more often referred to:

"Christology Today: Methodological Reflections." Originally published in Le Christ: Hier, Aujourd'hui et Demain. Edited by Raymond Laflamme and Marcel Gervais. Québec: Les Presses de l'Université Laval, 1976. Now also in A Third Collection, pp. 74-99.

"Natural Right and Historical Mindedness." Originally published in Proceedings of The American Catholic Philosophical Association 51 (1977). Now also in A Third Collection, pp. 169-183.

"Theology and Praxis." Originally published in Proceedings of the Thirty-Second Annual Convention (1977) of The Catholic Theological Society of America. Now also in A Third Collection, pp. 184-201.

There is also repeated reference to John Henry Newman, especially to the following works.

An Essay in Aid of a Grammar of Assent. London: Longmans, Green and Co., 1930.

An Essay on the Development of Christian Doctrine. New York: Doubleday pb, 1960.

Historical Sketches. Volume III. London: Longmans, Green and Co., 1924.

The Idea of a University Defined and Illustrated. London: Longmans, Green and Co., 1929.

PREFACE

A preface should provide a context for a book, and a context is a
remainder concept.[1] That is, in the present application, it would mean
everything relevant except the book itself. Further, what is relevant
divides under two headings: the subject-matter of the book, and the
author's purpose and activity in writing it, so that we have two waves
of relevance, spreading in concentric and widening circles from the
center to the immediate context and so to the very remote. That is why
we tend to write very long prefaces. Or, if we struggle to be brief, we
write and discard half a dozen before desperately and maybe irrationally
settling on one, any one, of the half dozen. The one I have finally
settled on will state the question this book tries to answer, the way I
hope to answer it, my reasons for thinking I can make a contribution,
and the real limits of that contribution.

The question regards the grand strategy of education and can be
indicated in a preliminary way by the extreme positions on two sides of
a recurring argument. Should education be a kind of banking procedure
in which the teacher hands over parcels of information that the pupil
duly stores in the safety-deposit box of the mind, and draws out as
occasion demands, especially the occasion of examinations? Or should
education be a freely developing evolution of inner resources, where the
pupil is put in a sandbox and left to grow in self-realization with the

---

1. I take this idea from Bernard Lonergan, "Hermeneutics. Notes for
   lecture during an Institute on The Method of Theology," Regis
   College, Toronto, July 20, 1962; see p. 14: "Context is a remainder-
   concept: it denotes the rest that is relevant to the interpretation
   of the text." These notes are not published as such, but they have
   been largely incorporated into chapter 7 of Lonergan's Method in
   Theology (London: Darton, Longman & Todd, 1972; New York: Seabury).
   For the Notes (and much other unpublished material) the reader may
   consult any of a chain of centers of Lonergan research: on this
   continent, at Regis College, Toronto; Concordia University, Montreal;
   The University of Santa Clara; and Boston College (this latter in
   process of being set up).

expectation that he or she will advance steadily from sandbox to, say, a
laboratory for nuclear physics?

     Extreme positions are caricatures, enabling us to recognize the
subject, but only through distortion of the salient features. For purposes of rational discussion we need a more sober statement, so let me
give the two sides as Dewey stated them after forty years of thinking on
the matter.

> To imposition from above is opposed expression and cultiva-
> tion of individuality;
>   to external discipline is opposed free activity;
>   to learning from texts and teachers, learning through
> experience;
>   to acquisition of isolated skills and techniques by drill
> is opposed acquisition of them as means of attaining ends which
> make direct vital appeal;
>   to preparation for a more or less remote future is opposed
> making the most of the opportunities of present life;
>   to static aims and materials is opposed acquaintance with a
> changing world.[2]

My question, then, on the basis of this lineup, is twofold: are these
opposed positions mutually exclusive, or are they complementary to one
another? and, if the latter, by what means can we unite them in one
productive process?

     With Dewey himself, and with my readers rather generally, I sup-
pose, this book will opt for the complementarity of the two. Indeed, I
regard that position as so evidently true that I do not propose to spend
very much time defending it; none of us believes in trying to clap with
one hand. The main point, then, almost the whole point, lies in the
second question: on what basis can we unite tradition and innovation,
gift and achievement, heritage and development, docility and personal
creativity?

     In general, when a controversy has run a long course--and this
one, it seems, has run a course of over three centuries[3] --what is
needed is not a refining of the terms already in use in the controversy,

---

2. Quoted by Thomas H. Groome, Christian Religious Education (New York:
   Harper & Row, 1980) p. 11.

3. Groome, Christian Religious Education, pp. 10-11.

but a pretty complete rethinking of the whole question, and the introduction of a new set of basic terms.   It is in this way that I hope to
answer our question on the strategy of education; specifically, by
making available in this field the fundamental rethinking Bernard
Lonergan has done on the problem of human development, and by introducing the set of terms he has evolved for the analysis of human
consciousness. In his view there are two directions of human development, inverse but complementary.   They can be called development from
below upward, and development from above downward.[4] The spatial terms
settle nothing, of course, but offer only a convenient pair of names and
a mnemonic image. The key lies in the structured route along which, in
either direction, development may travel, and this is provided by the
four interrelated levels of human consciousness: experience, understanding, reflection (and judgment), deliberation (and decision), four
levels concerned respectively with data, intelligibility, truth, and
values.

   If I think, then, that I can make some contribution to an old
controversy in education, my basis is simply whatever familiarity I have
gained with Lonergan's thinking over these thirty-seven years. The
creative element lies not in me but in my source. The validity of
Lonergan's thinking is in the long run a question for history to settle.
If any reader is unalterably opposed to his ideas, my advice would be to
stop reading at this very point. But really I am writing for those who
are already interested in Lonergan's thinking, who sense its power, its
fertility, its broad applicability, but who may be somewhat uncertain
how to make the transfer from ideas that are so fundamental, to procedures and materials that are so concrete as the education process. I
know that such people exist—they are out there waiting, educators who
are deeply interested in those fundamental ideas, and would welcome help
in extending them into their field; while I on my part have the same
interest from the side of Lonergan studies, for extending them into a
field so important, so crucial, so profitable, as that of education.

---

4. This pair of complementary ideas became fully explicit in Lonergan's
   thinking about 1974, and appears in some eight papers he gave over
   the next three years; see a partial list in my study, The Lonergan
   Enterprise (Cambridge, MA: Cowley Publications, 1980), p. 115, n. 37.

The obvious question for such readers is the exact relation of my contribution to Lonergan's own work on education; in particular, what relation do these pages bear to his still unpublished lectures of twenty-five years ago on the philosophy of education?[5] A simple and sufficiently accurate answer is that Lonergan's lectures stand to this book as chapters one to four of his Method in Theology stand to the next nine chapters.[6] The first four chapters of that book are a condensation of a lifelong attempt, under the headings of method, value, meaning, and religion, to bring Catholic philosophy forward into the twentieth century; the next nine chapters use that philosophy for a strategy of doing theology. Somewhat in the same way, Lonergan's 1959 lectures on education are an attempt to bring Catholic thinking forward and upward to the level of the times, and to lay down a consequent philosophy for education today. My own effort here will be to move from such a philosophy (which Lonergan has deepened and extended since 1959) to a strategy of education. It is the difference, I suppose, between a philosophy of war and the strategy of a military campaign.

The limits of my contribution on the philosophical side are, I hope, clear enough. Perhaps more important for educators are the limits on the side of what they rightly regard as their specialization. The list, if I spelled it out, would be extensive. The all-embracing confession is that I have no specialized training in this particular field. Nor do I think I should try to swot the material up in a kind of crash course. I look at books on education which deal with curriculum, extra-curricular activities, classroom techniques, audiovisual aids, methods for teaching this or that subject, scales for measuring progress, and so forth. I look at books on the psychology of education dealing with sex instincts, aggressivity, and the like; I look at books on sociology and the relevance here of tradition-directed, inner-directed, other-directed

---

5. The lectures were given during a two-week institute at Xavier University, Cincinnati, August, 1959. Tapes and recordings are available at the Lonergan Centers (note 1 above), where also will be found a typescript prepared for publication by John and James Quinn under the title: The Philosophy of Education. Lectures by Bernard Lonergan.

6. Lonergan, Method, chapter 1, "Method"; chapter 2, "The Human Good"; chapter 3, "Meaning"; chapter 4, "Religion." Chapter 5 outlines eight functional specialties which are taken up one by one (with two chapters for history) in chapters 6 through 14.

character, and so forth. And I am overwhelmed by it all. Surely it would simply show contempt for the expertise of professional educators and for the long years they put in to master their field, were I to set myself on a footing of equality with them because of some telescoped course of selected reading.

All the same one cannot write on the strategy of war without some acquaintance with tactics. And neither can I hope to mediate for educators between a philosophy and their specialized field, if I am totally ignorant of that field, and quite innocent of what goes on in the classroom. So what can I offer on that side, to limit, as it were, the list of my limits? Quite simply, it is my own experience at school, as a child, a boy, a youth, and even into adult years; in fact, I can say, not just facetiously, that it was around grade twenty-eight when I quit school. While this does not give me the expertise of a professional, it does give me a wealth of material detail which may serve as illustrations for my suggestions, as paradigms for my principles, as something of a test for the views I advocate.

Let me delay on that point a little, for I am concerned that the role of my own student experience in this volume be accurately understood. Its role is simply to provide material for that formal element which I hope to make my specific contribution. Over and over (more often than I realize, most likely) I will speak approvingly of the values and judgments formed in me by my schooling. So I should like to say here, once and for all, and as a blanket reservation on those repeated statements or attitudes of approval, that the point lies not in the values and judgments I learned, but in the procedures by which I learned them, whether the procedures followed the way of tradition or that of achievement. And those procedures are important simply as illustrating the constant factors of human development: experience, understanding, reflection, values, and the two-way traffic of their development as gift or as achievement. Much as a rural schoolhouse of 1921 differs from a metropolitan educational laboratory of 1984, it is my contention that the constants of human development are as much at home in the one as in the other. May I, however, express the doubt that this will really be a bone of contention with my readers? All I am doing is bringing to bear on education the precepts that Lonergan calls transcendental: Be attentive. Be intelligent. Be reasonable. Be

responsible.[7] Or, put a little less concisely: attend to the data, try
to understand the data, weigh your understanding on the scale of truth,
and allow your informed conscience to guide your conduct. To call them
transcendental precepts is to assert their universal applicability, and
who, in fact, would object to such reasonable and worthwhile advice?

        Nevertheless, I would warn readers that this reasonable and
worthwhile advice, which seems easy to accept in principle, may not be
nearly as simply to carry out in practise. In one sense it will change
nothing, but in a very fundamental sense it will change everything. It
will change nothing, or need change nothing in a good system of education, where reading, writing, arithmetic, and whatever, will continue to
be taught, and taught with the excellent techniques already in use. But
in a fundamental sense everything will change, for reading, writing,
arithmetic, and whatever, will all come under the domination now of a
philosophy of what we are and are called to be, and all of them will be
inserted into a grand strategy in which their ultimate purpose undergoes
reorientation. It is like the change from being an idealist to being a
realist; one sees and understands and speaks the same things in almost
every respect, but everything one says has a meaning now it did not have
before. I think educators, whose thinking is often dominated by notions
of curriculum, pyschology, techniques, grading, and so on, will find
that no small conversion--indeed, that a Copernican revolution--is
required to start thinking always in terms of experience, understanding,
reflection, and values. They may wonder whether the promise of this new
"system" warrants the effort. That is something they must decide for
themselves. I don't suppose there is any special reason why they should
believe me, or that I will help my case in any degree by prolonging this
preface.

---

7. For a brief presentation see Lonergan, Method, p. 20; for a fuller
   view consult the Index of that book, under "Transcendental(s)." If
   Lonergan's reasoning is correct, as I believe it is, the
   transcendental precepts would apply, not only to questions internal
   to education (curriculum, techniques, staffing, and so on), but to
   the whole movement of modernity to which works on education so often
   refer: questions of ecology, demography, sociology, culture,
   anthropology, and so on. In fact, I have found much under these
   headings in my readings on education, some of it profound, some of it
   radical, all of it stimulating; but I have found nothing that would
   render the transcendental precepts irrelevant.

One pleasant duty remains, though I can fulfill it only partially: to render thanks where thanks are due. My debts of gratitude will
appear from the book's history.   Back in 1979, Rev. James Nestor asked
me to talk to the Catholic Education Commission of Western Australia on
the relevance of Lonergan's thought to education.   The talk was revised
and repeated that same year in the Lonergan Workshop directed by Prof.
Fred Lawrence at Boston College.   Then, in the fall of 1982, Trinity
College, Dublin, and the Milltown Institute of Theology and Philosophy
jointly sponsored a more comprehensive symposium on the same topic, the
initiative in this case coming from Prof. J. Valentine Rice and Rev.
Raymond Moloney, respectively of those two institutions.   The symposium
too was repeated at Boston College, in the fall of 1983, and still under
the umbrella of the Lonergan Workshop.   With these stimuli and under
these influences, and with special advice from Rev. Desmond O'Grady of
the Milltown Institute and Rev. David Creamer of St. Paul's High School,
Winnipeg, the book gradually took shape, to be generously accepted by
Boston College for publication in their Lonergan Workshop Series. I am
greatly indebted to all those I have named, or referred to without name
as participants in symposium discussions.   I am likewise indebted to
those unnamed students of Lonergan's thought who have carried it forward
in the area of human development; it was impossible to undertake the
study their work deserves and still get what I had to say into print
under the space-time conditions that various life-factors set for us.

F. E. C.

February 1984

Addendum

Time marches on, and with it the debts of nations and authors
accumulate. Since I submitted my typescript to the "printers," the
circle of readers and critics has continued to grow. I have not taken
account of the further critiques, nor can I even list the further
readers, but I have to mention the late Rev. Gabriel J. Ehman, C.Ss.R.,
who, with youthful energy when he was almost blind and nearly eighty,
organized a symposium for educators in Edmonton in November, 1984, and

used my typescript and lectures as a focus for discussion; he will
remain for me a powerful argument for the efficacy of new ideas to keep
us young. I must record also my gratitude to Prof. Charles Hefling who,
in hours and hours of tedious labor, edited the work for publication;
and to Gilbert Cartier and to Paul and Paulette Kidder for the major
part of the typing.

One tries to pay such debts with a word of thanks, sincerely and
warmly expressed. But there is no way I can put into a word of thanks
my debt to Bernard Lonergan, himself gone to the Lord late in 1984. I
suppose the book itself, with my whole life of research and study, is a
word of thanks, in the Hebrew sense of a word that is an act and an act
that is a word. May this grateful act of mine not become a hindrance to
the understanding and acceptance of his ideas, or an obstacle to his
still ongoing apostolate.

May 1985

CHAPTER ONE

THE TWO VECTOR FORCES OF EDUCATION

The problem before us is to reconcile the age-old opposition in
education between the way of progress and the way of tradition. The
proposed solution will rest on the complementarity of two ways of human
development, which I will call the way of achievement and the way of
heritage. The way of achievement, to give it some preliminary description, is the way of progress under the dynamism of human consciousness,
of the drive to understand, to learn the truth, to respond to the deep,
interior exigencies of our intelligent and rational and responsible
nature. It is a drive that we experience; if we do not experience it,
there is no possibility of education. It is a drive that in some degree
takes care of itself, for it is spontaneous, it is our "nature," and one
may hope that, despite our incomprehension and errors, it will in the
long run muddle through to some record of achievement. That record
becomes in turn the inheritance of the human race, and so the second way
of development consists in handing on to later generations the accumulated patrimony of the community or nation or race. Although it is
received as gift, it is not to be conceived as a merely passive way, for
it is not appropriated without struggle; but the struggle is not, as it
is when we fight for a legacy, against rival heirs, but against the
stupidity and lethargy which is as much a part of our nature as is its
dynamism.

The two ways have been described as moving "from below upwards"
in the original development, and as moving "from above downwards" in the
handing on of development. The movements are explained as follows:

Development ... begins from experience, is enriched by full
understanding, is accepted by sound judgment, is directed not to
satisfactions but to values ...

... the handing on of development ... begins in the affectivity
of the infant, the child, the son, the pupil, the follower. On

> affectivity rests the apprehension of values; on the apprehen-
> sion of values rests belief; on belief follows the growth in
> understanding of one who has found a genuine teacher and has
> been initiated into the study of the masters of the past. Then,
> to confirm one's growth in understanding, comes experience made
> mature and perceptive by one's developed understanding ...[1]

So succinct a statement requires elucidation, which it will be the
business of this book to supply. For the moment let us simply note that
a single structure of human consciousness guides each process, the way
of progress moving from experience through understanding and judgment to
values, the way of tradition moving in the reverse direction from values
through judgment and understanding to mature experience. It is this
single structure, and the possibility of traversing it in either direction, that provides a real basis for the complementarity of the two
ways.

Metaphors are only metaphors, to be used so far as they illustrate a point and abandoned as soon as they become a source of
irrelevant difficulties. If, therefore, an elementary knowledge of
mechanics leads us to think of upward and downward movements as opposing
processes, as cancellation of one another, then it is time to abandon
this particular spatial metaphor of the dynamics of education. There is
indeed a conflict, as we well know, between the forces of progress and
those of tradition, in education as in other areas of human concern, but
it is not to be explained in terms drawn from mechanics.

And now, despite my last remark, I am going to introduce a second
metaphor, very directly drawn from mechanics, but one that may illustrate a little the possibility of two movements complementing one
another, even though they are to some degree in conflict. Above us at
the moment there are hundreds of orbiting satellites, neither shooting
out into space nor falling back to earth. To a rude mind, this is
mystery: what prevents the satellite from moving off into space? What
keeps it turning the corner, as it were, and so circling the earth over
and over? Alternatively, why does it not fall back to earth, as a stone

---

1. Bernard Lonergan, "Natural Right and Historical Mindedness,"
   Proceedings of the American Catholic Philosophical Association 51
   (1977), pp. 141-142. Reprinted as chapter 11 in A Third Collection:
   Papers by Bernard J. F. Lonergan, S.J., edited by Frederick E. Crowe
   (New York: Paulist Press, 1985; London: Chapman); see pp. 180-181.

does when I throw it up?   But, in an educated society, even a child
knows the answer: there are two vector forces in play; one would send
the satellite off into space, the other would cause it to fall back to
earth; the proper combination of the two, scientifically controlled,
keeps the satellite orbiting.   Similarly, perhaps, the twin forces of
progress and tradition may be understood in their own terms and so
controlled as to complement each other and contribute to the education
of the child.

        Enough of metaphors for the present point. This chapter has
three sections. The first will present the dynamism of human consciousness which lies behind the movement "from below upwards," but will do so
in the terms proper to human consciousness: experience, understanding,
judgment, values.   The second section will present the complementary
movement, again in the terms proper to the handing on of human development, where affectivity is the basis of values and beliefs, followed by
growing understanding and maturing experience.   The third section will
try to show the integration of the two ways. This is, of course, the
goal of education and so prior in intention to the two components. This
is to be kept in mind as we study these two components in somewhat artificial separation from one another.   A very useful guide here is
Maritain's well-known phrase, "Distinguer pour unir." We distinguish
elements, the better to understand the whole.

        The chapter is meant to be an initial overview of the whole book.
I am proceeding in the manner of geographers who provide a large-scale
map in which a small section is framed, with the frame then lifted out
of the whole and enlarged in a new map which shows that section in
greater detail.   Thus, the three sections of this chapter will be
expanded in chapters two to four, to carry our story up to the end of
secondary education. Then the whole process will be transposed to higher
levels in subsequent chapters.

1. The Way of Achievement

        Much of human achievement seems to be a matter of muddling
through rather than of steady progress according to a plan. Even the
church, in Chesterton's metaphor, is a coach lurching violently from

side to side as it careers wildly down the highway. One might despair
of finding any system, any settled basis, anything like constants, in
such a history. And yet, the very effort to suggest aids to education
supposes such constants. Whether the proffered aid be a philosophy, or
a strategy, or a set of helpful tactics, the authors (and there are
thousands) and their readers (many more thousands) implicitly affirm
their belief that there is something like a human nature which will
respond in certain determinate ways. Even those who reject the idea of
a human essence, who say only that people exist and must make of themselves what they are to be, implicitly affirm that people are such that
they can make of themselves what they are to be.

I believe that a great deal more than this can be said on the
constants of human activity, that there are levels of human consciousness which stand in a determinate relationship to one another and are in
fact operative in daily life from hour to hour. Still, it would be a
long story to distill these constants from the fuzziness of an ordinary
day with its ordinary events. I propose rather to illustrate my point
through the paradigm case of a simple courtroom scene. Here John Doe is
on trial for the murder of Richard Roe. A jury has been chosen, a dozen
witnesses have been examined and cross-examined, the opposing lawyers
have given their contrasting interpretations of the evidence. We await
now the verdict of the jury, and the action of the judge pronouncing
sentence or declaring acquittal.

This situation, colorless though our description of it be, can be
worked into a scenario of the highest interest for the present purpose.
The interest is not in any legal questions that might be raised: of them
most of us know next to nothing. Nor in the drama with which the scene
might be endowed by a gifted writer: on the contrary, I would wish here
to suppress that kind of dramatic interest and sketch events as tersely
as I can. No, the interest is analytic, epistemological, philosophical.
By that mouthful of words, I do not mean to restrict interest to the
professional group of those who think for a living, as if the case were
lacking in "human interest," the angle reporters look for in a story.
We all like to explain our actions; we all demand an account from others
of their statements; we all have a view of what we call "human nature."
In other words, we all deal in some degree with analysis, epistemology,
and philosophy. But ordinarily we do not, and cannot, and need not,

think with any precision on what we are and how we operate; we do not try to reduce our activities to fundamental categories, which we both distinguish from and relate to one another. That is just what this courtroom scene enables us to do, indeed obliges us to do, if we will think about the matter. We find that it sets out four operations in human affairs, distinguishing them very carefully from one another, but also relating them, so that the courtroom procedures from beginning to end move to a single goal. The drama, then, is philosophical; and, very conveniently, there are four "actors" or groups of actors, to play the different roles.

First of all, there are the witnesses, who are there with the very precisely defined role their name indicates: to bear witness, to give evidence, or—in the terms that I will find more useful—to provide the data for further actors and further operations. They are not asked to interpret the data, or to reach a verdict on the main question, still less to pass sentence. They are asked to testify on anything they have seen, heard, smelled, tasted, touched, or experienced, that may be relevant to the question. They are not even asked to determine whether the data they provide are relevant or not; if they attempt this, or go further to interpret or offer opinions, they may be quickly cut off. It is sometimes said that their part is simply to state the facts, but I find that way of putting it misleading. The one fact at issue is whether John Doe did or did not murder Richard Roe, and what the fact of that matter is, is not for them to decide. It is more accurate to say that they provide data for an explanation, and so eventually for a judgment of fact. If we use somewhat academic terms, and call that fact an item of history, subject to historical knowledge, then we could call the contribution of the witnesses "historical experience."[2] That term may seem strange to some of my readers, but in the total context, in which I wish to distinguish and then integrate the diverse contributions, I think it will make a good deal of sense.

The next actors to be considered are the two opposing lawyers, one for the defense, one for the prosecution. Their contribution too

2. See chapter 8 of Lonergan's Method, especially section 2, "Historical Experience and Historical Knowledge," pp. 181-184, and section 3, "Critical History," pp. 185-196.—I may owe this courtroom illustration to Dr. Philip McShane; if so, my warm thanks to him.

can be defined quite precisely.   It is not to give testimony, not to
pronounce a verdict, and again not to pass sentence; it is to give an
explanation of the data provided by the witnesses, and present that
explanation to the jury for judgment.   In the academic terms already
used, they offer "historical explanation" of the "historical experience"
recounted by the witnesses.   To that extent, they resemble historians
who collect data and ponder its meaning; indeed, to that extent they
also resemble scientists who observe phenomena in their laboratories and
construct a theory to explain them.   But the resemblance, I regret to
say, is limited. The true historian will test an explanation against
alternative views, will perhaps seek further data before coming to a
judgment on the question; the true scientist will distrust a theory till
a crucial experiment can be devised to settle the matter. But the
courtroom lawyers have taken their positions, or act as if they had
taken their positions, in advance of the verdict, before the truth of
the matter has been determined. Each works out an explanation to fit a
position already adopted, each examines and cross-examines witnesses
with the aim of giving verisimilitude to that position, each sums up his
or her case before the jury in an attempt to demonstrate the truth of
his or her explanation.

       An element of criticism has clearly entered my exposition, and I
would explain that before going further.   I am not, then, making an
ethical judgment on the two lawyers.   The prosecuting attorney may have
made a thorough study of the data before having charges laid. The
defending attorney may be convinced of the client's innocence, or justified on various other grounds for undertaking the defense. The whole
adversarial system, with lawyer pitted against lawyer, may be designed
to serve justice. On such matters, I will have something to say in
chapter five.   The present viewpoint is simply that of cognitional
theory, a philosophy of the human process involved in coming to know, or
arriving at the truth.   From that limited viewpoint, the procedures of
the lawyers have to be called an aberration: they are obliged by the
system to take part in what philosophically is a monstrosity. For they
must make opposed statements on a matter of fact, and in the very nature
of truth, one statement has to be false.   It has to be false, for the
positions are contradictory; even the modest statement, "It is not
proved," is contradicted by the statement, "It _is_ proved." In other

words, where due philosophical process calls at this stage for an
hypothesis or theory, which should be submitted, before judgment on the
truth of the matter, to reflection, further research, or experiment,
legal process calls for a position to be taken and pronounced true in
advance of the reflection which determines the truth.

Still, whatever our evaluation of these procedures, it may be
said that at least they provide the third group of actors, the jury,
with a clear pair of options to study as they play their role. Their
role, generally, is simple in aim: to say "Yes" or "No" to the question
of fact. And their judgment on this question, unlike that of the
lawyers, is legally and cognitionally definitive. That is, after
listening to the witnesses (in effect, assembling the data, gathering
the available historical experience), and considering the cases made by
the two lawyers (in effect, pondering possible answers to the question,
reflecting on the alternative historical explanations), they decide the
matter of fact: in effect, they contribute an item of "historical
knowledge," insofar as a judgment beyond reasonable doubt can be called
knowledge. I have said their role is simple in aim; I do not say it is
simple in execution. How they reach their verdict, and what the
implicit epistemology of their procedures is, are matters of the highest
philosophical interest, for they are called upon to decide a question of
concrete fact, and most of us know, from the four hundred pages of
Newman's An Essay in Aid of a Grammar of Assent, how delicate and
complex that operation can be. But perhaps there is no need, for my
present purpose, to go into that. Let us simply sum up by saying that
we have gone from historical experience through historical explanation
to historical knowledge.

Fourthly, there is the role of the judge. There is a compli-
cating factor here that we did not encounter when dealing with the
previous actors in our philosophical drama. For the judge has not only,
in a fourth distinct step, to act on the verdict of the jury, but also
to preside over the whole trial and all the procedures of the first
three steps. But, restricting ourselves to the final role, we can say
that the judge contributes the decision that turns a cognitional into a
performative process, that involves the action properly following upon
knowledge of fact. There is a minor difficulty of language here, for we
often speak, in perfectly good English usage, of the deliberation and

decision of the jury, and of the judgment handed down by the presiding
judge. But, if we take "judgment" and "decision" in their more precise
philosophical sense, then we will say that judgment belongs to the jury,
and decision to the judge.   This latter role may seem simple to understand and easy to play; but let us note at once, since I wish to use the
courtroom as a paradigm for human activity, and decision is so important
an element in our lives, that judges do not merely rubber-stamp a jury's
verdict. Their role is quite distinct, with its own procedures and its
own norms, as appears not only in their guidance and decisions on procedures throughout the trial, but also in the deliberation proper to
sentencing (where often they have wide leeway) or in their evaluative
remarks accompanying either sentencing or acquittal.

One more point before we begin reflection on our paradigm. It is
easy to add here, though it may not enter ordinary cases of law, a fifth
and somewhat different operation, namely, the exercise, on the highest
level of authority, of an act of mercy.   I remember dropping into a
courtroom as a boy, not yet at the midpoint of my teens, just as the
jury on a murder trial filed in to declare its verdict, "Guilty, with a
recommendation of mercy." Sentence of capital punishment was mandatory
at that time, but the recommendation was eventually acted on, and the
penalty reduced to life imprisonment.   Now, years later, I vividly
recall the judge's question to the jury, "On what grounds do you
recommend mercy?"   Vividly too do I recall that poor old recluse
standing in the dock, friendless, bewildered, on trial for an act of
rage to which he was provoked, and I reflect soberly, gratefully, that
the law is not inhumanly rigorous, that it does yield to considerations
higher than those of its own code of justice. "On what grounds" indeed
does any of us survive our stupidities, our moments of weakness, our
rash judgments and foolish acts, except those of a humanity, a humane-
ness, that is not achieved by legal or philosophical processes, but is
given from above?   This kind of reflection is not just a personal
reminiscence; it is very much to the purpose of this book, and I will
return to it in our next section, and still more fully in chapter three.
But it seemed important to introduce it here, lest the procedures of a
lawcourt, so artificially distinguished, so legally determined, seem a
poor paradigm for the areas of human living that are more familiar,
areas in which love and mercy play so dominant a role.

The artificial character of courtroom procedures is not, of course, to be denied. It is indeed that very artificial character that is instructive, that provides an illuminating, if schematic, view of much that we do habitually in daily life. For all we achieve begins with what we see and hear or somehow experience (for the moment I speak only of "outer" experience). Not content, however, to be passive receivers, we are curious about it all; we wonder why things happen the way they do, so much so that life without wonder is in a high degree boring. We sleep and dream, and wonder what the dreams mean, if anything. We wake and wonder what causes the shimmering light we see on the ceiling. I notice a lump on my neck as I wash, and perhaps a nameless fear erupts: what could the lump be? I hear a cryptic remark from the boss as I arrive at work: what did it mean? And in answer to all these questions, ideas form; sometimes they leap to the mind, sometimes they result from long pondering. But ideas are not the term of the process, for we may and likely do form several ideas which exclude one another: could it be this? Could it be that? Is there a third explanation? The very multitude of possibilities compels us to distrust our ideas. So, thirdly, we are driven on to reflection, weighing the evidence, arriving at a state of mind in which we can pronounce one idea right and the others wrong, in which we know, with probability or certainty, the right answer. Then, on the basis of our knowledge we may be led to take certain decisions. Many daily decisions, it is true, seem thoughtless, but that only means they are based on habitual knowledge; in the normal process of human achievement, it is regarded as highly irresponsible to choose blindly, or through prejudice, rather than reasonably, in accordance with what we know.

It is the courtroom scene, I would insist, that in its very artificiality brings into clarity the procedures of daily life. I believe that William James has said that the world of the baby is "a great, blooming, buzzing confusion."[3] R. S. Lee, to whom I owe the quotation, goes on to say that "all is blurred—sight, sound, smell, and feel— rather like a picture badly out of focus."[4] What these psychologists

---

3. Quoted by R. S. Lee, Your Growing Child and Religion (New York: Macmillan Publishing Co., 1963), p. 50.

4. Lee, Your Growing Child and Religion, pp. 50-51.

say about the sense-world of the baby, I would be inclined to say about
the consciousness, the "inner" world, even of the adult: experience,
understanding, reflection, decision—they are a confused whole; it is
only certain critical events that force us to distinguish elements that
are really distinct all the time.   But a courtroom case is just such a
critical event, separating the four steps and allowing us to discern the
proper object of each step in the whole process: data assembled on the
level of experience; an intelligibility discovered in the data, often
with a counter-intelligibility that challenges our first understanding;
the truth of the matter, or the real facts, what is actually the case;
and finally the level of values that guide our decisions and measure our
actions.

I am sure that students of Lonergan are yawning over this exposition of the four levels; I certainly yawn over their expositions, and
even over those of Lonergan himself, when he is obliged to run through
the four levels again. But I think too that most of us realize that,
under cover of words and phrases too familiar now to excite us, there
are very fundamental realities to be grasped, and that those realities
are profoundly significant, for daily life as for academe, for perspective on our history as for prophetic insight into our present. And
perhaps our courtroom scene will serve to bring that home to us if we
look at it in historical perspective.   What a contrast it offers to
those dark ages in which trial by ordeal settled the question of guilt.
What a contrast it offers to those dark moments in our nominally
enlightened age, when lynch law and the frenzy of a mob take over the
judicial process. What a contrast even to the legalistic manipulation
of the judicial system by which shyster lawyers attempt to prostitute
the law. The contrast in all cases is with the four transcendental
precepts as listed by Lonergan: be attentive, be intelligent, be reasonable, be responsible.[5] Perhaps the contrast will help us realize better
the profound significance of an analysis we run through too perfunc-
torily. Perhaps also it will serve to make us grateful for the procedures of law and order that our founding fathers and mothers, the
framers of our constitutions, the prophets and legislators of our way of
life, have thought fit to articulate in the four acts of our courtroom

---

5. For a brief presentation, see Lonergan, _Method_, p. 20.

drama. At any rate, I hope my exposition will help newcomers to
Lonergan's thought to see something of the analysis of human consciousness which he has worked out after long pondering.

Analysis is done for reintegration: again, Maritain's "Distinguer
pour unir." So let us add now that the four activities, for all their
distinctness, form a close natural unity, a unity we implicitly recognize in speaking of the artificiality of their separation in the courtroom. And I am not speaking now of the original unity of the blooming,
buzzing confusion, the unity of daily living, of the give and take of
ordinary conversation, where the four functions mix and mingle in a
medley, and we make a nuisance of ourselves if we insist too much on
their distinctness. No, I am speaking of a unity of goal and purpose.
All four levels head for the same goal; in the courtroom for a specific
decision, in daily life for the full deployment of our conscious
resources. And I am speaking of the natural sequence which knits them
together in a conditioned series. The lawyer needs the testimony of the
witnesses to make out a case; the jury needs the lawyer's explanation,
needs differing explanations, in fact, to form a judgment; the judge can
make a decision ordinarily only on the basis of the jury's judgment.
That is, if we look at the sequence from the viewpoint of later steps,
we will say that they are conditioned by the earlier ones. But equally
well could we see the series from the viewpoint of earlier steps, and
then we would say that the earlier call forth the later: what a
mutilated system it would be that stopped with the uncritical testi-
monies of the witnesses, or the conflicting presentations of the
lawyers, or the simple statement of fact by the jury.

One last note to obviate a possible confusion. When I speak of
four separate actors, each with a distinct function to perform, I do not
mean that witnesses do not form ideas of their own, or make judgments of
their own, or hope for a certain sentence. And similarly, I do not mean
that the other actors in the drama operate on one level only in their
interior activities. But I am saying that what is accepted and admitted
into the process is just one specific contribution from each actor.
Each has an appointed activity; and it is these appointed activities
that are so carefully distinguished, and by their very distinction are
capable of making a definite contribution to the unitary process.

Let us sum up, a little more technically, this long exposition.
We have been talking about human nature, in its conscious orientation to
and pursuit of goals and objectives. We have noticed a dynamism at
work, unfolding in successive activities that reveal a structure and are
exercised with the kind of regularity and inevitability that belong to a
"nature." The structure has four levels, which we may call the empirical (that on which data are received, grouped, recalled), the intelligent (on which we ask why, form ideas), the reasonable (on which we
reflect, test our ideas, form judgments, reach the truth), and the
responsible (the level of values, on which we take action in accordance
with an informed conscience). We can also name them the levels of
experience, understanding, reflection, and values. This latter set of
names I find convenient, for the initial letters give us the useful
acronym, EURV. And this turns out to be especially useful when we wish
to reverse the process and talk of values, reflection, understanding,
and experience, for then we have the acronym, VRUE. It is, in fact,
that reverse direction that will occupy us in our next section.

2. The Way of Heritage

If my readers are willing to accept our courtroom scene as a kind
of paradigm for basic human operations, as a kind of analysis of human
process that is not abstract and theoretical, but concrete and operational in practise, they may also agree that we could go on from this
concrete analysis to a more theoretical statement of what we are and how
we act. That is, this concrete analysis in which the composite is
actually broken down into distinct elements, may validate in general the
four levels of human activity, the natural sequence in the structure of
our operations, the relation of operation to operation and of level to
level, and the unity of the whole complex psychological mechanism. But
the same readers may not be so willing to accept the paradigm's application to the purposes of education. Not even adult life, they may argue,
will benefit through being directed according to this model. It may
well give us a kind of X-ray of adult activity; but it is not X-rays of
our life companions that we carry in our wallets or set on our desks,
rather it is color photos. Just as it is not legal procedures that

guide our dealings with others, but the swift give and take of unstruc-
tured conversation. Now, if adults are not ready to live according to
this model, much less will children be ready to learn that way.

There is truth in this objection, and much more than a grain of
it. We do not generally converse according to the courtroom model. I
do think conversation would often benefit from a better grasp of the
distinction and relations of experience, understanding, reflection, and
decision, but I know the havoc wrought in conversation when we habitually use the manners of a cross-examining lawyer.   I know it well,
having learned it the hard way; I still remember, vividly after forty-
five years, the remark of a candid friend: "You argue as if your
opponent wanted to be shown his error."   So how can we expect children
to distinguish data from explanation, explanation from fact, fact from
consequent decision? They have no understanding yet of life's ways, no
viewpoint from which to judge wisely on the world and themselves, no set
of values with which to guide their decisions. They lack even the most
basic element, that of experience itself. To impose courtroom distinctions, sequences, procedures on their living and their learning would be
to encumber the vigorous young David with the heavy armor of Saul (1 Sam
17:38-39).

Yet surely there is more to be said than that. Surely a structure of consciousness that is built into human nature, that unfolds in
so natural a sequence, has something to do with the life of the child
and with its education. I believe, of course, that it has, and that the
solution to our puzzle lies in adding, to this natural upward direction
of development, another movement that Lonergan calls development from
above downward, the one that I propose to call the way of heritage, of
gift, of tradition. Let us look again at the lines we have made our
motto-text:

> the handing on of development ... works from above downwards; it
> begins in the affectivity of the infant, the child, the son, the
> pupil, the follower. On affectivity rests the apprehension of
> values; on the apprehension of values rests belief; on belief
> follows the growth in understanding of one who has found a
> genuine teacher and has been initiated into the study of the
> masters of the past. Then, to confirm one's growth in under-

standing, comes experience made mature and perceptive by one's
developed understanding ...[6]

The sequence, we notice, is just the opposite of the one that obtains in
the courtroom; instead of experience, understanding, judgment, and
values, with each based on the previous member, we have values and judgments, understanding and experience, in a descending order. The two
movements may be diagrammed as follows:

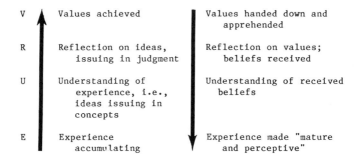

V	Values achieved	Values handed down and apprehended
R	Reflection on ideas, issuing in judgment	Reflection on values; beliefs received
U	Understanding of experience, i.e., ideas issuing in concepts	Understanding of received beliefs
E	Experience accumulating	Experience made "mature and perceptive"

The arrows indicate the main dynamics of development, upward from
experience, downward from tradition. But the diagram is simplified; for
example, there is a horizontal dynamic as well as a vertical: in the
left-hand column values issue in decisions, reflection issues in judgments, understanding in concepts, experience in the vast and various
world of images that is the mind's treasury. Further, in the downward
movement, judgments may be formed by reflection on values, or simply
received in function of the value of believing. And so on.

Now the downward movement, which is our present concern, is said
to be the "chronologically-prior phase."[7] Not only is it first in time;
development is more "fundamentally," more "importantly,"[8] from above

6. Lonergan, "Natural Right and Historical Mindedness," A Third
    Collection, p. 181.

7. Bernard Lonergan, "Theology and Praxis," Catholic Theological Society
   of America, Proceedings of the Thirty-Second Annual Convention
   (1977), p. 15. Reprinted as chapter 12 in A Third Collection; see p.
   196.

8. Bernard Lonergan, "Christology Today: Methodological Reflections," Le
   Christ hier, aujourd'hui et demain, edited by R. Laflamme and M.

downward. This may seem strange to the reader, who might wonder how there can be movement at all in this direction. I suggest that there are psychological reasons, especially for Lonergan students, for finding it strange: we have given so much time and energy to study of the way from experience to idea, from idea to what "is," from "is" to "ought," and given so little to the opposite movement. But reflection will show us that the unity of consciousness is prior to its components, and so the communication between levels is prior to the direction that communication takes. Further, we have a wealth of experience on the way an idea already grasped enables us to call up appropriate images to illustrate it, experience too of the way an intellectual apprehension of the mysterious can set one's spine tingling,[9] that is, experience of the downward way. In short, we should not set pseudo problems in the path of our understanding.

It is more to the point, I think, especially in a work on education, to grasp the reasons for the priority of the downward phase. They are ready at hand, some in the ontological order, some in the psychological. Ontological reasons, first of all. To put the matter in Thomist terms, what the child is given in the fourfold structure of consciousness, is something like potencies, but the potencies await actuation. A Kantian would say, I think, that the child is given something like empty forms, and the forms need filling in. In Lonergan's terms, there is given initially a dynamic structure which can be defined by basic terms and relations; then the need in development is for derived terms and relations to give the procedures of daily life, of common sense, of mathematics and science, of art and philosophy, and so forth. So, ontologically, there is a further building to be done on the fundamental framework, a realization to be achieved of what is not yet in being. And this, of course, takes time; it is a matter of slow growth, of directed effort, of persevering application. There seems a need for gift to precede achievement.

Gervais (Québec: Les Presses de l'Université Laval, 1976), pp. 48, 50. Reprinted as chapter 6 in A Third Collection; see pp. 77, 79.

9. See Insight: A Study of Human Understanding (London: Longmans, Green and Co., 1957), chapter 17, especially "The Sense of the Unknown," pp. 531-34.

Existential factors confirm the point.   For the human good in
general, and human development in particular, results from the right and
happy combination of many elements: a correct orientation, a choice of
proper means, attention to varying circumstances, etc. But the whole
enterprise may fail due to a deficiency in any single element in this
combination: "bonum ex integra causa, malum ex quolibet defectu."
Biblical wisdom tells us of the two ways before us, the way of life and
the way of death, the way of good and the way of evil. But this does
not mean the chances are about even for success or failure; as far as
the basic situation goes, the chances at any time seem weighted in favor
of failure. And the child has the further problem that, while its
"animal" nature develops naturally, and some of it very rapidly, getting
off to a head start, its "higher" nature has to be cultivated long and
perseveringly; it starts life, one may say, with a mortgage against
success.

If all this sounds pessimistic, so does the old and well-established doctrine of original sin, and what I have been saying is not
irrelevant to that doctrine. Still, we do manage to muddle through life
and history with a fair degree of success, with a respectable batting
average. So the question will be, How do we do it? What turns the odds
around to give hope, to let success win out over failure? One may
appeal to the old Scholastic doctrine of habits: well-formed habits
greatly improve the odds in favor of success.   Of course they do; but
then Catch-22 comes into operation: how do we form these good habits?
Obviously by persevering in the right way over a period of time; and for
that perseverance, we need the habits in advance. Catch-22 turns out to
be no joke.

All this may seem an excess of dialectic, but it was important to
convince ourselves that the natural built-in structure of human consciousness is not by itself a guarantee of successful living, and that
it does not by itself provide an adequate basis for educational procedures. Now, however, let us leave dialectic and move to what we all
know perfectly well is our way out of the impasse we have constructed.
Namely, that besides original sin, there is redemption; besides the
habits that we slowly and laboriously cultivate, there are the gifts of
the Holy Spirit that God gives us in abundance; that, besides the way of
human struggle for achievement, there is the way of heritage and gift;

or, to return to the ideas with which I would structure this book, besides development through experience to understanding, judgment, and values, there is development in which values and judgments are communicated in an atmosphere of love and trust, to guide us while understanding slowly forms to render experience mature and perceptive.

I wish to sketch this way of development, not in the detail reserved for chapter three, but in overview, a counterpart to the one provided in the opposite direction by the courtroom model. It will not be as sharply outlined, as carefully structured; it is not the nature of this way to be so well articulated. That is why we had to begin with the way that proves artificial in comparison. But, with that structure now at hand, I think we can discern the general lines of a development from above in a process that would otherwise seem haphazard.

Where shall we look for a model for this movement, to make our discussion as concrete as possible? Most frequently, Lonergan takes up the matter in the context of love of God, and then he will say that development from above downward is effective through "the transformation of falling in love," and "in the measure that this transformation is effective." He will add, "There has begun a life in which the heart has reasons which reason does not know."[10] But perhaps the love we have for God does not supply quite as vivid a model for everyone as we would wish. And we remember the statement I have already quoted twice, that this movement "begins in the affectivity of the infant." Let us add another very general statement: "Basically this process rests on trust and belief."[11] Now I do not know any simpler, better, more universally experienced setting for that situation than home and family. So I propose to take as model a very ordinary home. I have to visualize it as particular, and I suspect that it will look rather like a rural home of sixty years ago, but that does not mean that this sketch is autobiographical—only that it aims at being concrete in the measure that is possible for me. And I hope that in such a description the reader, any reader, may find the universal elements of education in the way of heritage.

---

10. Lonergan, "Christology Today," A Third Collection, p. 77.

11. Lonergan, "Theology and Praxis," A Third Collection, p. 197.

Imagine then an old-fashioned home; an ordinary number of ordinary children; ordinary parents for whom divorce is about as unreal as a trip to the moon; siblings who quarrel and fight as most siblings do, but are basically obedient and well enough behaved; a frugal home, where there is no cold or hunger, but no luxuries either; a home where the children are trained to help, each with chores to do; a home where there are games, especially in the long winter nights; where there is reading, if not much stimulating conversation; a religious home, where there are scenes of the Last Supper and the Crucifixion, where family prayers are said, the Rosary even, if you would be really old-fashioned.

Reflect now what it means to say of a child in such a home that "the handing on of development ... begins in ... affectivity," that on this affectivity "rests the apprehension of values; on the apprehension of values rests belief; on belief follows ... growth in understanding" and finally "experience made mature and perceptive." The basic force, then, is love. No one, I suppose, will dispute that, though many families are not demonstrative about it, and frequent breaches of the peace do occur. But the basic fact comes through, most obviously when there is a death in the family, and the loss of sister or brother brings a grief that is nothing less than a physical pain. It comes through again in the shock, the word is not too strong, the shock of horror the nine-year-old pupil suffers when he or she reads in English history of brother actually going to war with brother for a throne or a dukedom. That such things could be at all in a family had been entirely beyond his or her horizon, and enters it now as a profoundly disturbing reality.

The source of this love is also beyond doubt. It comes from the parents, beginning in their total commitment to one another and extending to their children, to include them all in one strong circle, to make of the home a single unit, knit together by manifold bonds, bonds of common interests and concerns, surely, but still more bonds of an affection that finds its object rather in the family as a whole than in individual members. This love of parents the children learn to reciprocate; cor ad cor loquitur in mutual exchange; and prior to all exchange of messages, words and deeds of love, there is the gift of love itself.

If we ask what children learn in such a home (we are including now the third level of consciousness), we may think first of obvious skills, ways of speaking, and so on.   We learn to tie our own shoelaces and to say "Please" and "Thank you," and maybe there doesn't seem to be much difference in those lessons.   But   reflection reveals far deeper lessons, lessons of value and meaning, attitudes and views, that become part of us and guide our conduct for years, maybe throughout life.   The lessons may be only implicit, the guidance may be only that of a remembered scene or event, rather than that of a precept, but the influence is nevertheless real.

There is a wide spectrum of such lessons of value and meaning. They may start with simple matters like the lesson of order: order in the day's timetable, in the care of one's possessions. They may teach one the role of comradeship, lifting one above self-centered pleasure in the simple joy of going fishing with one's father. They may advance to the humble virtues of family or village togetherness in the sharing of tasks and possessions, in the development of responsibility to the community. They may reach a deeper level in respect for people, simple people, all people, the nobodies of the community, but especially for the old and feeble, a respect suffused with warm affection when the elders are uncles and aunts or (happily, for many children) grandparents. They may include reverence, awe, before the mystery of death, a deepening of one's attitude to life, of one's acceptance of world and life and time, and of their limits.

If we ask how communication takes place in this learning process, our first answer may be negative: these lessons are not learned by rote from books or from precepts, not primarily. "Values are caught ... more than taught," I read in a recent article.[12] There are indeed parental corrections (the importance of a rebuke for communicating values is widely overlooked, and the oversight is serious), but the correction is not the motive force; that resides in the power of example in a setting of love and trust.

The communication of religious values is a good illustration. The love that is a trust, that bathes the child in an atmosphere of security, also surrounds father and mother with an aura almost of divinity. They are after all the eternal ones, forever grownup, there

---

12. Tim Bentley, "Values: Where do Children Learn Them?" United Church Observer (Toronto), June, 1982, p. 27.

from the beginning; they are the almighty ones, the providers, who can do anything, who do not need to ask others if they can stay up late, if they can have another dish of ice cream. Until, of course, the child notices that Mamma and Papa do ask Someone else; until it sees these mighty pillars of a fixed and stable society kneeling in prayer, until it sees them afraid in the awful lightning storm, as the father goes from room to room with holy water, repeating "The Lord will bless us and save us." In some such way, surely, along paths and in steps I will leave to religious psychologists to trace, in the interaction and mutual clarification of event, and word, and gesture, the child finds images and words and actions and something like a concept through which to relate to the transcendent.

This reference to religion serves a double purpose, illustrating the formation of both values and beliefs. Basic, surely, is the communication of a transcendent value, a value before which father and mother are no longer sovereign rulers of their choices, a value communicated to children more by example than by word, and received on their part through the trust in which they hold their parents, rather than by doctrines taught and convictions verbally expressed. But values accepted in trust will be followed by judgments accepted in belief. The child hears the word, God, learns at length to ascribe some vague meaning to the word, a meaning based on the actions that accompany its use, and so very naturally asks questions about this "God": who is he? How old is he? Where does he live? Has he a wife? And what parents answer, received in trusting belief, becomes part of the child's stock of "knowledge," its set of views, its way of looking on the world and life and time, of seeing all things in the perspective of their creation by Someone who is greater by far than any of them.

What I have illustrated from religion holds for the range of the child's interests and concerns. The "value" represented by the great knowledge parents possess is the basis of the child's acceptance of the many judgments parents communicate to it. There may indeed be judgments formed directly by the child itself on the basis of the values it has accepted; but the vast majority of its judgments are accepted indirectly on the basis of the value obscurely apprehended in believing one who knows.

The whole process of learning and development in this direction
is too unitary, compact, obscure, for us to articulate it distinctly
along the four steps of VRUE—values, reflection, understanding, and
experience. But the general direction is discernible and clear enough.
It is clear, for example, that the child's values and judgments are not
formed on the basis of personal experience, for experience is largely
lacking. It is clear too that the child has not yet the developed
understanding to provide a cognitional basis for the judgments it holds
and the values it accepts.   There is the need to understand, emergent
and expressed in the perpetual "Why?" of the child (if it is a real
"Why?", and not just a word the child has learned to use in imitation of
older persons); but even though the "Why?" cannot really be answered at
this stage, the child continues to maintain its world of views and
values.

So the sequence seems to be from love and trust through values to
judgments and some understanding.   With growing understanding one's
experience is "made mature and perceptive."   There is a sense also in
which the child's experience may be directed by the parent to correspond
to the values and judgments transmitted.   That is, a whole new world of
experience, in the wide sense of the word, is opened up in the pictures,
games, books, movies chosen by parent for the child. There is even a
sense in which the child constructs its own experience to correspond
with his or her little world of judgments and values. Thus, I still
remember the time when, on hearing thunder, I thought of God up above
the clouds turning the handle of a machine which gave out this rolling
noise. Surely I had been told that God makes the thunder, and surely I
associated this action with that of my Uncle Ernie turning the handle of
the cream separator when I visited his place on the farm. But I formed
the image for myself, answering a need that still exists and is only
imperfectly met by the public liturgy of the church and the ancient
images of the scriptures.

We have not yet reached the point of talking about formal education, but perhaps there are already discernible the lines of a strategy
of education that would move by way of gift and tradition from above
downward. Though I have taken an ordinary family as model, I have not
conceived the family narrowly. It extends to a wider circle of rela-
tives, extends also to the community of neighbors. And this is highly

important; the very expansion of a friendly world, even before I learn
any views or values from it, is itself an education: to find that the
world contains so many interesting people (just when Papa and Mamma may
be growing a bit dull too!), people who do wonderful things, like sawing
wood with a machine, or shoeing horses, people with a different kind of
cookie in the pantry, or strange artifacts on the mantle, maybe a ship
inside a bottle.

Above all there is the impact of books, which expand beyond all
dreaming the world of the child, limited so far to family, or clan, or
community and village. What magic casements those books are, opening on
the foam of perilous seas! What mysterious lands those ships go sailing
out to discover! What incredible adventures await the traveler! And
let us remember too the important fact that the people the child meets
in these books are not just new faces and names; they are also new
characters, delineated now in a way that never occurs in its immediate
world. There are strong silent men; there are noble and secret benefac-
tors; there are those who struggle against misfortune—new characters by
the score.

This then, is the way of development from above downward, the way
of heritage, of tradition handed on, the way of gift to stand in lieu of
an as yet non-existent achievement, but also to inspire later achievement. It is truly the fundamental, the chronologically prior way of
learning.

3. The Resultant Unity

We have studied human development on the basis of two quite
different models: the lawcourt, and the Christian home. We have set
forth the two ways in artificial separation from one another, as if each
took its own direction without any relation to the other. But that
raises a third and all-important question: how do we get the two of them
together again? Life is not lived out in two directions, or under two
warring influences--not comfortably anyway. No more is the child going
to be properly educated by being pulled apart by two influences. As
life is one, then, so is the educational process, and this third section
has to join together what analysis has put asunder. Distinguer pour
unir.

Our two models do not themselves offer any obvious clues to a solution: what institutions are more badly paired than a lawcourt and a Christian home? But let us return to the overall image I proposed at the start, that of a satellite orbiting the earth. Here we have one definite path, the resultant of two quite distinct vector forces. It is a path that is understood only when the two forces are analyzed and depicted on a graph; and, very important, it is a path that is only controlled when the two forces are understood separately and the proper force of propulsion applied to balance that of gravity. I repeat, this is only a metaphor, with the limited uses of a metaphor. So let us not ask more of it than to be a helpful image and possibly a stimulus to questions.

The real solution, then, to the problem of integrating progress and tradition in the field of education, has to be found in human nature itself, in the constants of the structure of consciousness, and in the variables of its development. Here we come to the most critical point of our inquiry. There will be general agreement that we cannot simply jettison tradition in favor of progress, or jettison progress in favor of tradition; somehow the two must work together for the good of the child, pupil, student—yes, and citizen too. But if this book said no more than that, we could not possibly justify adding it to the tens of thousands of books we already have on education. What it offers, and what I believe to be a distinctive offering, is the possibility of uniting the two ways in a single development of human consciousness, and that on the basis of a fundamental view of the levels of consciousness and the two-way traffic between levels. The appeal, then, is not to any possible integration of content in the curriculum, and not primarily to any possible complementarity of technical methods of education; it is primarily to the interiority of the educand, to the subjectivity of the human subject who is learning, not to the academic subject which is being taught, and so it supposes a whole philosophy of that human subject.

Let us then pull together the various remarks already made on human consciousness, its structure, its operations, and its two-way traffic. Altogether fundamental is the unity of consciousness: it is not a matter of one compartment feeling and another thinking; it is "I" who both feel and think. Fundamental also are the levels of conscious-

ness: to see with the eyes is not to understand with the mind, a high
I.Q. does not necessarily endow one with wisdom, "is" is not the same as
"ought." Fundamental likewise is the communication between levels,
and—the crucial point for my purpose—a communication that may move
from A-level to B-level as easily as from B-level to A-level. This is
surely the natural consequence of a unity of levels in consciousness,
but it is equally a matter we may verify empirically, if we only admit
all the data available to us and do not arbitrarily exclude the greater
part as being merely data of consciousness. That is, we are aware of
questions that carry us from sights and sounds to ideas, from ideas to
judgments, from judgments to decisions and values; and similarly we can
verify in our own history the process from shared values to judgments
accepted in trust, judgments we struggle to understand; understanding in
turn affects our experience in many ways, notably in the sense of the
uncanny (shivers along the spine) that accompanies apprehension of the
beyond, but more commonly in the way habitual understanding calls up
appropriate images or instances to illustrate an idea.

In such a view of how we are constituted and how we operate,
there is nothing to prevent development from starting at either end of
the structure, to proceed along a given path and arrive at the other.
That is, it may start with sight and sound in the infant and progress
through understanding and reflection to judgments and values that are
its own achievement; or it may start with a heritage of values and
judgments and proceed through growing understanding to more mature
experience. As values may be created, so also may they be handed on; as
judgments may result from weighing the evidence, so also may they be
accepted in trust; as understanding may puzzle over what is observed, so
it may puzzle over what is believed to be true. Of course, there will
be the possibility of conflict as we work toward the collaboration and
unity of the two ways; as progress must take its start from tradition,
so tradition must submit to the critique of progress. But, in principle, the development achieved through personal experience and the
development based on accepting a heritage can be conceived as complementary to one another. The all-out war between opposing approaches can be
transformed into peaceful cooperation, once there is a sufficiently
fundamental analysis of human operations to accommodate both and assign
to each its role.

With our simplified preliminary view, then, let us think of an
outer-directed aspect, or an input from tradition, and an inner-directed
aspect, or a self-generating element from the unfolding and developing
dynamism of human consciousness. It will be the educator's business so
to encourage the self-generating element, which starts slowly, and so to
moderate the input from the outside, which dominates at first, that the
path of the pupil is one of steady transition and maximum progress. All
a philosopher-theologian can do is set down general principles and aid
heuristics with the stimulus of further questions. I suggest, then,
that the educator think of the initial situation as one of peaceful
coexistence but no real unity of forces. There is overwhelming input
from tradition, with the forming of at least implicit values and judgments, along with training in skills, the use of tools, and the like.
From the start, of course, there is the accumulation of experience, the
effort to understand, with questions striving for formulation. But in
the early stages experience is shapeless, and wonder is not specified in
precise questions; it is more a matter of

> Children's faces looking up
> Holding wonder like a cup.

Again, criticism is not so developed as to offer any more than momentary
opposition, and the spontaneous "piety" and docility of the child soon
prevail over the beginnings of self-assertion—I doubt that there are
any "born rebels."

I suppose next that I am only stating the obvious to note that
the period of most painful opposition is that of the adolescent years.
For now experience has accumulated, questions come thick and fast, there
is a developed understanding, there is training in the use of words and
of argument, and elders may learn from bitter experience how dangerous a
situation they have created for their own dominance by putting the
weapons of words and argument into the hands of those still inex-
perienced in life. For the young can hardly know how undeveloped they
are in personally formed judgments and values; their physical growth,
their arrival at puberty, lead to the natural but inaccurate analogy of
a parallel development in mind and heart; and so they are ready for
rebellion. The reactionary and arbitrary conduct of elders can easily

aggravate the situation, which rapidly becomes explosive. There is no
remedy for this, except for parent and teenager, each in his or her way
and in the measure possible to each, to understand what is going forward
and be reasonable and responsible in dealing with each other.

        I suggest, thirdly, that in the final stage, after these painful
years of conflict, the mature person reaches a state of relative equilibrium, of real integration, of resultant unity of the vector forces,
in which the influences that were at first merely coexisting and later
conflicting, are now in some balance, at peace with one another. This
can be depicted in a graph.

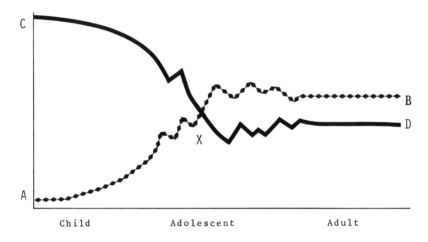

The line, AB, moves along a base that measures years of life but rises
on the graph to show the increasing importance of personally achieved
development; the line, CD, moves along the same time base but descends
on the graph to show the decreasing importance of development that
depends on tradition.   The two lines become jerky as they near one
another, cross at the point, X, which ordinarily occurs in adolescence,
and then follow erratic paths for a while till they achieve some equilibrium, represented by the parallel lines of a further development that
combines heritage with achievement.

        On the basis of this analysis, the task of the educator will be
to aim at the equilibrium of maturity, to be intelligently aware
throughout the years of the two forces at work, and intelligently

practical in promoting each, and so to estimate the development of the
pupil as to make an intelligent adjustment of the two, and reduce, so
far as may be, the violence of the period of conflict. That phrase, so
far as may be, is important; we are dealing with free persons, persons
whose freedom is coming to birth; we cannot manipulate them like robots.
But surely it is clear that the pupil must be brought to an understanding of the two forces at work, and to some realization of their
relative schedules of operation.   No rigid rule can be laid down for
everyone here, as will appear from the following comparison of two
extreme cases. Is there a school in which a disproportionate emphasis
is put on the self-development of the pupil, on one's thinking and
deciding for oneself?   Then tradition will suffer; pupils will be
deprived of a great deal of their rightful inheritance; they will reach
the adult stage (I do not say "maturity"), with sharply trained minds
that can go for the jugular in debate, but with impoverished and under-
developed views and values. Is there, on the contrary, a school where
information is handed out in packages, where the questions of budding
intelligence are nipped off, where no exercise of responsibility is
allowed? Then the school is attempting to turn out Yes-persons; Yes-
persons have a habit of becoming violent No-persons, and in any case the
graduate is ill-fitted to take his or her place in a changing and ever
developing world where intelligence, judgment, and responsibility are
called for. Obviously, one will give exactly opposite pieces of advice
to two such schools.

      Obviously, too, we must get beyond such generalities if we wish
to say anything useful. In the following chapters I will say what I can
from the side of the methodologist, but in the end of the day, it will
be the educators themselves who must make the detailed input. Meanwhile, before closing this chapter, I will appeal, in support of its
general drift, to a statement on "the true way of learning" by the great
Newman. He has been talking of the extreme positions which we may call
those of credulity and skepticism, the one represented by acceptance of
tradition, the other by exercise of the Cartesian doubt (though Newman
does not here refer explicitly to Descartes).   He makes a plea himself
for what he calls a "reasonable scepticism" but then goes on to put that
plea in perspective:

Of the two [credulity and skepticism], I would rather have to
maintain that we ought to begin with believing everything that
is offered to our acceptance, than that it is our duty to doubt
of everything. The former, indeed, seems the true way of
learning. In that case, we soon discover and discard what is
contradictory to itself; and error having always some portion of
truth in it, and the truth having a reality which error has not,
we may expect, that when there is an honest purpose and fair
talents, we shall somehow make our way forward, the error
falling off from the mind, and the truth developing and occu-
pying it.[13]

Lest we think Newman a bit naive on the prospect of error falling away,

we should also remember his involvement in academe and recall his

profound thinking on the role of a university. Thus, he asks, "What is

a University?" and answers:

It is the place ... in which the intellect may safely range and
speculate, sure to find its equal in some antagonist activity,
and its judge in the tribunal of truth. It is a place where
inquiry is pushed forward, and discoveries verified and per-
fected, and rashness rendered innocuous, and error exposed, by
the collision of mind with mind, and knowledge with
knowledge ...[14]

It would be hard to overestimate the debt we owe to Newman on the role

of a university, or more generally on the process of thinking and

judging. But I do believe that Lonergan, building on Newman's genius,

has given us a more precisely articulated organon to control university

work in the four specialties of research, interpretation, history, and

dialectic, built on his own analysis of human consciousness into

experience, understanding, reflection, and decision. But there are also

the four specialties of foundations, doctrines, systematics, and commu-

nications, likewise built on that analysis, which would be Lonergan's

transposition of Newman's road of acceptance, "the true way of

13. John Henry Newman, An Essay in Aid of a Grammar of Assent (London:
Longmans, Green and Co., 1930), p. 377.

14. John Henry Newman, Historical Sketches, volume 3 (London: Longmans,
Green and Co., 1924), chapter 2, "What Is a University?" See p. 16.
I owe the reference to John Tracy Ellis; see his contribution, "A
Tradition of Autonomy?" in Neil G. McCluskey, editor, The Catholic
University: A Modern Appraisal (Notre Dame: University of Notre Dame
Press, 1970), pp. 232-33.

learning." Development at the university stage will not concern us
specifically till chapter five, but meanwhile I wish to note that the
first four specialties pertain at that stage to the way of personal
achievement, just as the four levels in their upward movement pertain to
it at any stage of development; similarly, the other four specialties of
university life pertain to the way of tradition, gift, heritage, as the
four levels do at any stage in their downward movement.[15]
Progressivists are apt to deplore the second way as a vestige of
medieval ecclesiolatry, and traditionalists to view the first as the
gateway to unbridled skepticism. My hope is that the following chapters
will enable us to see more clearly the need and role of each.

---

15. There will be need in chapter five to make this statement more
    precise.

CHAPTER TWO

EDUCATION AS ACHIEVEMENT

There is a real difficulty in talking, in two distinct chapters, about education as achievement and education as heritage, and thus separating for thought, elements that ought to be united in reality. But that difficulty is insurmountable: we cannot analyze without distinguishing ideas; we cannot set forth ideas except one at a time, in a sequence that we hope will keep the relationship clear and allow the unity to emerge in the end. So all I can do here in this regard, is ask the reader to wait and judge chapters two to four as a unit.

There is a distinct further difficulty when I make education as achievement the prior consideration, and deal with education as heritage only in a subsequent chapter, for the way of heritage and tradition is the chronologically prior way of learning, and might therefore claim prior study. This difficulty is, of course, avoidable: one has only to switch the order of the chapters, which is of my own choosing. But I justify my choice by the clear correspondence of achievement with the four levels of the structure of consciousness, now sharply defined. The way of tradition has levels indeed, but they do not show up as a succession of clear-cut plateaus; the way of achievement is, or can be, just such a succession. To start with the latter, therefore, will enable us to proceed from what is clear to what is more obscure, mostly a profitable direction to follow.

To say that the steps of development from below upward are clear is not to say that they are self-evident or automatically achieved. But it is possible to see them clearly now through the labor of generations of thinkers. For a roughly sketched history we may think of Plato for the distinction of the intelligible from the experiential, of Aquinas for the distinction of the factual from the intelligible, of Kierkegaard for the distinction of the self-involving from the factual. Those are only headlines from history, with the inaccuracy that belongs to headlines, but they are an index of the slow groping of humanity down the

dark corridors of consciousness. To use again one of my favorite metaphors, at the end of the corridor we can turn on the light and see the
route we have traversed. But, having done so once, why not avail ourselves of the light, and walk no longer in darkness? That is my justi-
fication for taking the route, experience, understanding, reflection,
values, in the hope that we can thus illuminate the reverse route of
values, reflection, understanding, experience.

      One further preliminary note: there is a considerable difference
between the four levels in early years and the same levels at university
or in one's life career. The basic functions do not change, nor does
the basic relationship of one level to another; these are the constants
in the otherwise changing world of the learning subject. But the
materials on which we operate are different, and there are nuances in
the exercise of the four basic functions, nuances which develop with the
subject. From this latter viewpoint, Lonergan contrasts the world
mediated by meaning with the child's world of immediacy:

> Now [i.e., in the world mediated by meaning] mere experiencing
> has to be enhanced by deliberate attention. Chance insights
> have to submit to the discipline of the schoolroom and to the
> prescriptions of method. Sound judgment has to release us from
> the seduction of myth and magic, alchemy and astrology, legend
> and folk-tale ... Most of all we have to enter the existential
> sphere, where consciousness becomes conscience ...[1]

This may be further illustrated on the first level by the nuances of
difference among the three terms, experience, data, research. All three
pertain to the first level, but we will think of the child as experiencing in simple wonder, of the advancing student as looking on experience
as data to be understood, of the researcher as assembling data with
technical precision in order to make a single contribution to an academic enterprise. This will become clearer in chapter five, which will
deal with the university world. Chapters two to four will have to do
rather with primary and secondary education.

---

1. Bernard Lonergan, "Christology Today," A Third Collection, p. 78.

1. Data and Their Assembly

We begin our schematic treatment then in the order of natural achievement, starting with experience, going on to understanding, to proceed later to reflection, and so to decision and values. The first thing to note is that in the present analytic approach experience is considered simply as data for understanding, as oriented to a higher level, as material for inquiry. The child collects experience all day long (at nighttime too, if it dreams), and this experience has a value in itself; it can certainly become, under parent or teacher, a vehicle for meaning and value. These aspects we shall consider in due course. But for the moment, we are taking a particular view of experience. We are considering experience as "deposited" in the data bank of memory (let us not utterly scorn the "banking" concept), where indeed it is a treasure to be recalled with joy, but also raw material to serve the further purposes of intelligence. It is the latter aspect that belongs in this chapter, and we ask, then, what such storage of experience means to the educator, what techniques, ideas, judgments, decisions, it suggests to him or her.

Let us first explore the notion of a data bank. Think therefore of the data a child collects very early in education: the basic tools of the learning business, such as the letters of the alphabet, or the numerals for counting. This collection does not yet provide data for understanding (who understands the funny shape of the letter 'a'?), but it will illustrate the notion of a bank of retrievable data. To go from the simple to the simply primitive, let me tell you about my childhood data bank for the alphabet: it was present in my imagination as a rather irregular semi-circle rising from 'a' on my left to curve through 'l, m, n' at the top and descend to 'z' on my right. It derived, I suspect, from having had a porridge bowl with the twenty-six letters around the rim; since we cannot easily read upside-down letters, the circle got opened out in my image into a semi-circle. To continue our exploration of the primitive mind, let me tell you also of the pattern I used both for the sequence of numbers and for my daily prayers: it had somewhat the shape of a big 'S.' The numbers set off from left to right along the bottom arc of the 'S,' at about twelve they swung sharply back up

the middle of the arc, and at twenty they turned right again along the
top which grew much longer than symmetry would approve till it got to
about fifty; here the route became vague. Curiously, my recited prayers
followed the same route, the "Our Father" and "Hail Mary" corresponding
to the bottom arc of the 'S' (and to numbers one to twelve), the "God
bless Mamma and Papa" (and a lot of other people) taking us back on the
middle, and the long Apostles' Creed, with Acts of Contrition, and so
on, swinging us along the top of the 'S' again. It's my guess that this
odd route was my child's picture of the road that set off for Grand-
mother Mahoney's place, one of special importance to me as a child, one
therefore that was a natural mnemonic for sequences that were not in
themselves memorable. The arc I used for the alphabet departed for
special reasons from the pattern, but the irregularities it suffered
were perhaps an attempt to reduce the two patterns to one; even the
child's imagination may have reductionist tendencies!

     I hope this venture into reminiscence has not bored my readers.
What I want to suggest, and a concrete example seemed the best way to do
it, is the potential of the notion of memory as a data bank, where
experience can be somewhat systematically stored and more or less
readily retrieved. No doubt educators have scores of devices that are
more efficient than mine were; no doubt children with different mentali-
ties will need quite different devices, maybe musical melodies rather
than spatial images; possibly too, computers and calculators have elimi-
nated some of the need for this use of memory. All I want to suggest is
a certain potential in the notion.

     The importance of this emerges when we go on from those quite
arbitrary tools which are the funny marks used for letters and numbers
to the still largely arbitrary but now immensely fertile field of
language. For, however arbitrary the meaning of given words, there is
still a type of understanding involved in grasping their meaning and
use. To learn to say, along associative paths which I need not study
now, that I "hear" the "music" but "see" the "sunset," is to have
acquired some understanding, one that Lonergan calls an understanding of
names if not of the realities to which they refer (scientia nominis, not
scientia rei, in Scholastic terms).   Our question now becomes: what
methods can we devise for storing in retrievable fashion the wealth that
words represent to the child? I am not thinking now of words as music
to the ear, which are stored in the memory through the power of melody,

or words as releasing fantasy which are stored through remembered nursery rhymes and fairy tales, or words as vehicle of the beautiful which are stored with the help of rhythmic poetry. All these are of incalculable importance in education, but they belong rather to my next chapter. I am thinking rather of words as data for understanding, as having a particular meaning, not maybe in the one-to-one correspondence we find in a reductionist dictionary, but as meaning something fairly specific nevertheless. How are we to collect and store this wealth? One may think of memorizing long lists of words and meanings. But one may think also of reading, reading, and reading again those authors whose use of language recommends itself by its clarity, precision, and wealth. Experience (of ourselves and of others) surely points to the latter as the better way, as does the modern philosophy which insists that the meaning of words resides in their use rather than in the abstraction from use that simpler dictionaries present.

More important still than learning the meaning of particular words, and far more of a peak experience, is grasping the very notion of words as having a meaning, that is, coming to understand the meaning of meaning itself. Lonergan illustrates this by the deeply moving story of Helen Keller, born blind and deaf, but brought by an extraordinary teacher, through repeating an experience over and over, to associate a certain touch with a specific touch-meaning, until one brilliant moment, in what was surely a giant step for mankind, Helen got the idea: this particular touch-sign given by her teacher "meant" this experience. She had learned in that one moment, not only the "word" for "water" but the very notion of signs with a meaning. For she went on at once to "ask" for a multitude of other "words" under which to classify her various tactile experiences. Some of us may recall less spectacular but equivalent events in our own childhood. I have a most vivid memory of one day standing beside my mother, with my "First Primer" open on the little table where she was busy at her own work, and still, over the years, I recapture the peak experience of that moment. I can explain this only on the analogy of Helen Keller's experience: that there was born in my mind, at that moment, through some explanation my mother gave me of my little book with its simple words and pictures, the very idea of language. I hope readers will be able to recall similar experiences of their own; surely the recall would have a potential for the work of education.

I have been anticipating somewhat, bringing in ideas that pertain
more directly to the section on understanding. But that had to be, if
we were to grasp the notion of experience as data for understanding, and
this in the crucial area of language. To return to the level of data as
data, we should note here that language has the effect of extending
indefinitely the range of experience and intentionality. Let me present
this in Lonergan's words:

> However, as the command and use of language develop, one's world
> expands enormously. For words denote not only what is present
> but also what is absent or past or future, not only what is
> factual but also the possible, the ideal, the normative. Again,
> words express not merely what we have found out for ourselves,
> but also all we care to learn from [others].[2]

That is, not only this typewriter before which I sit, but also the distant land of China belongs to my world of meaning; not only my neighbor
whom I hear tramping about in his room, but also Jesus of Nazareth; not
only our solar system which I in some sense see, but the God also whom I
cannot see. The universe of language becomes a world of data for
thinking of and affirming, in short, for mediating realities on which
data may be only indirectly available, as is the case with China, or not
available at all, in which case a word, God, is linked with a religious
experience orienting us to mystery.

With this consideration a more important question emerges,
related to our question on devices for storing data, as strategy is to
tactics. It is the question of selection: what data in the untold
wealth available are to be chosen for storage in the child's data bank?
The problem is not one of storage space: it seems we have some ten
billion brain-cells for that purpose, many of them never used. The
problem is rather one of the time and energy available and how best to
use it. If my memory is correct, the young Adolf von Harnack was
reading the church fathers in Greek at the age of eight; and, thinking
of that, I reflect how immeasurably richer was his data bank when he
came to the study of theology than was mine. But then I read also that
someone is in the Guinness book of records for having memorized the
value of pi to several thousand decimal places. And, reading that, I

---

2. Lonergan, Method, pp. 76-77.

reflect that at least I did not store my data bank with as many stupidities as some others did: I never learned pi beyond 3.14159.

   I think this notion of the memory as a data bank for life may
have helped bring home to us how very fundamental and strategic are the
educator's decisions on the early content to feed into the child's
memory. To have given language a role of overwhelming importance is
already an instance of such strategic decision. To modify that choice
in a new world of television, computers, and God knows what other technical creations, would be another instance in the same genus of strategic decision. And how should we modify the tradition in this matter?
It would be foolhardy for me to offer advice to educators with their
long experience and painstaking study of these questions. But I cherish
the old-fashioned hope that language will never be dislodged from its
place of honor. The hope too—to anticipate chapter three for a moment-
-that the kind of poetry which it is possible to memorize may never be
banished from the schoolroom; let unmemorizable modern poetry flourish
as it may—I realize that

           all sorts of things and weather
      Must be taken in together
           To make up a year and a sphere

—but only let traditional poetry not disappear from the child's patrimony and heritage.

   Among the thousand questions that spring to mind here, one at
least seems to fall more within my terms of reference: it is the question of heightening consciousness through the use of drugs. How does
this relate to that human development which we are tracing through the
four steps of experience, understanding, reflection, and decision? I
set aside the medical question of the harm that might ensue to the
nervous system, though of course that is relevant to the moral question.
The moral question is naturally crucial and the moralists will surely
ask what input our methodology can make to their problem. First, then,
all experience is, or can be, oriented toward understanding; in this
respect, what is experienced under the influence of drugs does not
differ from other experience: is it intelligible? if some intelligibility emerges, can it be tested in reflection? and so on. Next, there
are experiences that at the moment impede the further unfolding of the

psychological dynamism; in this respect, experiences under drugs can be related (I do not say, equated) to the ecstasy of sex experience (as the medieval Scholastics used to say, after Aristotle, "In coitu omne animal caret intellectu": In the act of coition no animal, not even the human, can exercise intelligence). Thirdly, there is experience in itself; in this respect, experiences under drugs can be related (again, I do not say, equated) to jogging, daydreaming, whistling, or chewing gum. With such considerations, I do not pretend to have settled all the questions that either the moralist or the educator may raise; but the categories I suggest seem the relevant ones from the present viewpoint. Further, even an amateur moralist can now discern the ambiguity of the term, heightening of consciousness. Consciousness is fourfold: experiential, intelligent, rational, and responsible. To heighten experiential consciousness alone (as happens in a nightmare) is not the highest of goods; to heighten it at the expense of destroying intelligent, rational, and responsible consciousness raises the key moral question.

To sum up this section of the chapter: we have been considering the level of experience in the child as a basis for the further step of understanding. A strategic decision for the educator then becomes the storing of experience as data, and I suggest the analogy of a data bank as offering ideas for exploiting this feature of the child's intellectual equipment. There will then be decisions to make about the selection of data, about the effective manner of storing it, of the ready retrievability of the data and so on.

But I must insist on the present limited perspective. Experience is not just "useful" for understanding, something to be collected for further achievement at a higher level. In the old classification we have the liberal arts and we have the useful. Besides the category of the good, there is the category of the beautiful. And we have only to think of the riches that pour into the child's mind and heart through songs and games, through nursery rhymes and stories, through pictures and puppets and clowns and circuses, through the companionship of playmates and teachers, to realize how very one-sided the present approach is. But one-sided though it be, it too has its place and role. Understanding is important; and understanding requires data. There is an unfolding set of operations, and so we proceed to the second in line, the level of understanding.

2. Understanding

Understanding, I believe, is the Cinderella of the four levels of human consciousness, neglected to a degree that escapes culpability only through ignorance of the structure of consciousness. So that, if I had to recommend to educators concentration on only one of the levels, this is the one I would choose. In fact, to some extent, the other three can be depended on to look after themselves, though they may do so carelessly. That is, data are going to be collected one way or another in any case, and widely, except in the sad case of autistic children. Judgment and decision are going to be called forth often just in the demands of daily living, though they are illegitimate children in the way of achievement if exercised without understanding. But the place and need of understanding in the composite of human activity can so easily escape us. I say this with a certain sad irony, having just read a university-level prospectus which makes much of the critical methods in use at the school (in effect, stressing the exercise of judgment) but does not say a word about understanding. My advice, then, to educators, would be: stress understanding, insist on it; in the phrase from the Pastoral Letters, argue, obsecra, increpa, coax, persuade, cajole, motivate your pupils; one way or another make the point, in season and out of season.

I do not say, Communicate understanding, for that is not possible in any direct way. One can communicate values and judgments, so I believe, in the way of tradition (chapter three); but understanding is a wholly interior event, immanently generated, personal to the individual pupil. Still, it depends on a definite dynamism, it aims at a definite goal, it follows a definite route in the total cognitional process. If we know something of these matters, we will find devices by the hundred, as good teachers have always done by natural talent, to assist, in the manner of Socratic midwifery, at the birth of understanding.

Let us clarify here what we mean by the words (synonyms, really), understanding, intelligence, insight. We do not mean "information," as might be the case when we talk about the intelligence branch of foreign service in the government. We mean what Lonergan describes in the instance of detective work: "reaching the solution is not the mere

apprehension of any clue, not the mere memory of all, but a quite distinct activity of organizing intelligence that places the full set of
clues in a unique explanatory perspective."[3]

In further clarification, we may notice also that we do not mean
the act of generalizing from experience which is so common—so human, we
might say—but is an act which Thomas Aquinas attributed to the vis
cogitativa, and located on the sensitive level. Generalizing of this
type is really a matter of collecting in the imagination instances of a
kind. In Aristotle's example, a practical nurse knows that this remedy
will cure this ailment (the Thomist quia), where the doctor knows why it
will cure (propter quid for Thomas). And nurses know simply because
they have seen repeated instances of it, even though they do not understand its nature or operation.[4]

Everyone can think of hundreds of examples of this exercise of
generalizing. Let me relate one from my own past. I had been studying
a year in Rome when a fellow-Canadian arrived there. We went one day
for a walk, and presently my companion said, "The Roman women don't wear
hats, do they?" (This was long ago, when hats were the mode back home.)
I reflected for only a moment before replying, "That's right; they
don't." The point is that I had been in Rome a whole year, without
making this generalization, without "collecting" in my imagination these
many instances of hatless Roman heads. My observant companion did it in
a few minutes.

Such generalization shows a tendency innate in us, an extremely
useful capacity, one moreover that is relevant to understanding in that
it provides the natural setting for wonder and for a possible insight.
To be observant in this way might lead one, for example, to wonder why
Roman women didn't wear hats thirty years ago, and maybe to discover
reasons which one could convert into a good hat business. But educators

---

3. Lonergan, Insight, p. ix.

4. The question here is of a process that I call "generalizing from
   experience." This by no means excludes a generalizing which is a
   genuine act of understanding—as I would suppose the General Theory
   of Relativity to be, and would claim Lonergan's Generalized Empirical
   Method is also (see Insight, pp. 72, 243-244).

have higher aims than the hat business, and so I would ask them, broadening our base: could we not make better use of this remarkable power that leads so directly to understanding? Could there be classroom exercises to bring it to the pupil's attention? And what controls should one incorporate into its exercise to prevent the hasty and invalid generalizations to which we are prone? I am not ready with an answer to such questions, but I conceive it to be my task to suggest them to educators, on the ground that so valuable a power ought not to lie dormant in the slower pupil or go untrained in the keener.

But such generalizing is not understanding, and the latter is our direct concern. Our aim here is to help the pupils help themselves, for which purpose we have to know how understanding works. What then makes understanding work? The answer, or a clue to the answer, is at hand empirically (this is Lonergan's broader use of "empirical") in the data of consciousness: we have a built-in dynamism, a drive toward understanding, in our sense of wonder. It is part of our natural equipment, and in that sense acts spontaneously, as in the child's exuberant and continual "Why?" But it can become stunted, due to a too sensual life, a too tyrannical teacher, or other causes. Even when active it needs to be guided into areas where it can operate effectively, so that the pupil does not become frustrated. There are many stages between the child and the dedicated scientist, but the wonder of the one may become eventually the persevering inquiry of the other, which Lonergan describes as follows:

> It can absorb a man. It can keep him for hours, day after day, year after year, in the narrow prison of his study or his laboratory. It can send him on dangerous voyages of exploration. It can withdraw him from other interests ... fill his waking thoughts ... invade the very fabric of his dreams ... demand endless sacrifices.[5]

In between there is the pupil, to be encouraged to wonder, to be directed along paths where his or her wonder can be effective, and, eventually, to locate his or her capacity for wonder in the total process of development.

Again, it does not lie in my competence to suggest detailed tactics, but only to provide the kind of help I have called heuristic,

---

5. Lonergan, Insight, p. 4.

which consists mainly in asking leading questions. May we not, then,
engage in a better give and take with those who make education a matter
of problem-solving, learning from their techniques, but perhaps providing them with a philosophical base and incorporating what is positive in
their program as we exploit the child's natural wonder? May we not
propose questions and then simply wait a notable time, allowing them to
lie like seed in the fertile mind of the child, instead of rushing in
with the answer? Why is Holland called the Netherlands? Why does ice
float on the lake when it is just frozen water? Why do the coasts of
South America and Africa face each other like pieces of a jigsaw puzzle
to be fitted together? May we not go a long step beyond problem-solving
to encourage problem-raising? That is, having primed the pump with
myriad questions, may we not find ways to help pupils raise their own
questions, discover their latent power for questions, and develop it?
No doubt, it will look odd on the pupil's report card, "This pupil got
'A' for 'wonder,'" and the teacher may suffer the scorn of those who
haven't the faintest idea of what is going on; but that is a small fee
to pay for the privilege of being Socrates to the young—Socrates himself paid more dearly.

      Wonder, however, only begins the process. It is the operator and
prime mover of the enterprise; but on what material does it operate?
Here we may draw on the advice of St. Thomas Aquinas: we understand, he
says, what is understandable, in the image; we cannot even think without
calling up an image. In his way of putting it: "Anyone can experience
the following fact for himself, that, when he would understand something, he forms images to represent the case, and in these images he
seeks and finds the desired 'insight.'"[6] The material on which wonder
operates is therefore the image. Already we have a principle so simple
that few bothered much with it till Bernard Lonergan resurrected it from
St. Thomas and Aristotle, and wrote on it under the sub-title, "Insight
into Phantasm,"[7] but one also so powerful that it is the key to every

6. Summa theologiae, I, q. 84, a. 7—freely translated.

7. In articles that first appeared in Theological Studies, 1946-1949;
   they were later published under the title, Verbum: Word and Idea in
   Aquinas, edited by David B. Burrell (Notre Dame: University of Notre
   Dame Press, 1967). On "insight into phantasm," see especially pp.
   25-33 of Verbum.

act of understanding. Namely, we do not understand by comparing concepts, or scrutinizing principles, or deducing conclusions, not in the
ultimate instance anyway; we understand by the simple and pedestrian
device of forming an image in which to study the problem.

We seem to have abandoned the usage of our first section, where
we talked of "data," and introduced by stealth a new usage, that of
"images." But the relation between the two terms can be clarified
easily enough for present purposes.   "Data" is simply the Latin plural
of "given" (the French "donné"): what we receive through eye, ear, and
so on, what is not our own creation; "images," however, are free, we can
form them as we will, while remaining on the level of experience, for
they are always material for understanding. This difference shows up in
the mathematical examples used by St. Thomas (Lonergan did not invent
the use of geometry to illustrate the act of insight). Two simple problems: to prove that the interior angles of a triangle are together equal
to two right angles; and, given a triangle inscribed in a semicircle
with the diameter as base, to prove that the angle opposite the base is
a right angle. The problems are of no importance; what is supremely
important is St. Thomas's advice for solving them: to draw the figure
and actuate its potential divisions.[8]   In simpler English: produce
sides, bisect angles, inscribe circles, draw parallels, in short,
keeping trying possibilities, shuffle them around, till the idea leaps
into the mind. He does not say what divisions to actuate, what possibilities to shuffle around, for the simple reason that we do not know a
priori what they are; there is no logic of discovery in Thomist insight,
one simply keeps trying till the fertile figure occurs. In Lonergan's
words again: "Stare at a triangle as long as you please, and you will
not be any nearer seeing that its three angles must equal two right
angles. But through the vertex draw a line parallel to the base, and
the equality of alternate angles ends the matter at once. The act of
understanding leaps forth when the sensible data are in a suitable
constellation."[9]

---

8. In IX Metaphysicorum, lect. 10 (numbers 1888-1894 in the Marietti
   edition).

9. Lonergan, Verbum, p. 14.

Another way of putting this might be: give the imagination free rein. A freely roaming imagination is a basic condition for understanding, and it is just here, in fact, that differences begin to appear between lower and higher animals. But the human animal has a new capacity and new goals to attain: an imagination that roams in search of understanding. At first, there may be no signposts, but eventually we stumble on one. Or, to change the metaphor, we shuffle the data as one would shuffle a pack of cards, to see what comes up. But, as we grow in mastery of a field, mere shuffling gives way to creative maneuvering. A geometry teacher, for example, will think of various devices: let the figure be a parallelogram; suppose the base is fixed, but the four corners are hinged; suppose we swing the whole figure on its fixed base—what ideas emerge as we see it moving from side to side? And so on.

Geometry offers clear-cut and simple images. But images vary: they may be simple, complex, detailed, schematic, symbolic, abstract—varieties multiply. Language may call up associated images, or it may have become by long use so pregnant with meaning as to serve in itself as an image and basis for insight. The point to remember is that the intelligibility is immanent in the image, or in the shuffled data, or in the schema, or in the field obscurely represented by the schema. The image is not just a catalyst.

Let me illustrate this by contrast. In a detective story I read years ago, the sleuth had collected a great deal of data but could not find the solution. One day he sat in a restaurant and began to draw concentric circles on the tablecloth, making them smaller and smaller till he reached a mere point. Then he leaped to his feet with his version of Eureka; he had found his solution. Maybe he had, but I doubt that the circles on the tablecloth had anything directly to do with it. They may have provided data for the geometry of circles, or for the problems of laundering linen. But they had nothing to do with his problem of finding the murderer.[10]

---

10. This may be the place to mention what Lonergan calls "inverse insight," which "apprehends that in some fashion the point is that there is no point" (Insight, p. 19); and the still broader category of the empirical residue—for example, particular places and times (p. 26). I am not sure when pupils will be ready for such ideas; in general I suppose they are ready when they ask questions that require these ideas for an answer.

One last point on this level of understanding. Understanding, to be useful, to be communicated, to become part of science, must be expressed. And the expression must be clear conceptually. Concepts must be defined, and definitions must enter into logic. There is a whole apparatus of learning here, which I am not going to discuss. I do not deny its importance. Clarity is a wonderful virtue in thinking, coherence is equally a virtue in statements, and rigor a virtue in inference. The reason I do not discuss these matters is that ordinarily they get quite enough attention in the school; certainly in philosophy they get a lion's share, to the great detriment of understanding.[11] Perhaps then I may suppose the educator has means at hand for exploiting this side of the pupil's development.

I began this section with an almost impassioned plea for attention to understanding. I have developed the idea in a rather general way. But I would not conclude without stressing the fact that most developments of understanding are particular. So the educator has the task of choosing the areas for the exercise of intelligence—which amounts to choosing the subjects on the curriculum. Not much can be said on that here, but a useful principle might be that the pupil's understanding will not develop unless he or she can handle the data. This he or she can do for simple arithmetic, algebra, and geometry; and so these subjects lend themselves to training in understanding. But the very young pupil cannot manage the data of history; he or she simply lacks the experience for it. One sees how questions expand in all directions and how little I have tried to do in this section. But I do hope that an idea of the importance of attending to understanding has been conveyed.

---

11. See Lonergan's campaign for intellectualism against conceptualism, Verbum, passim (see the Index). On the clarity, coherence, and rigor that should characterize logic, see Bernard Lonergan, A Second Collection, edited by W.F.J. Ryan and Bernard J. Tyrrell (London: Darton, Longman & Todd; Philadelphia: The Westminster Press, 1974), pp. 50, 170, 197-199, 201-202.

3. Judgment

If understanding is the Cinderella of human operations, the
activity of judging is one of two favorite daughters, the other being
the activity of deciding. All day long we are busy judging, often with
praise or blame included to mingle fourth-level acts with third-level.
And, so far from deploring this reveling in the exercise of judgment, we
encourage it. Youth are urged to think for themselves, which doesn't
always mean really to think, but only to have views on widely ranging
questions, either without thinking at all or without thinking with the
depth required by the subject-matter; thus, the winner of a lottery is
questioned for his views on shoes and ships and sealing wax, or a beauty
queen for her views on cabbages and kings; and, in a more academic
setting, a university prospectus will make much of the critical spirit
fostered in its student body.

One would expect, with such universal devotion to the practise of
judgment, that formation in the capacity to judge, and the conditions of
exercising judgment, would have high priority in our schools, that
pupils would be taught the nature of the judging power, have explained
to them the conditions of possibility of judging, be instructed in the
practical limits of judging, be exercised in "practise" judgments; one
might even hope, without really expecting it, that teachers would go to
the extreme of stressing the difficulty of forming a really rational
judgment, and of inculcating a certain humility in regard to one's own
judgment. But does such training occur? I invite my readers to reflect
on their own schooling and answer for themselves. How often was judgment mentioned as a capacity that might be trained? Or "good judgment"
set forth as an ideal? As something possibly more important than a high
I.Q.? Discussion was of course encouraged (rightly enough, if perspective is maintained), but training in judgment? Really! As for a class
project of making a judgment, one can imagine the shock waves that might
run through a community if that were proposed, parent telephoning parent
in alarm, "Did you hear about the eighth grade's project? They are
going to make a judgment! A judgment, for heaven's sake!"

The pity of it is that the act of judging carries such a heavy
responsibility. Understanding can be counted as innocent fun; we can

try, without any personal commitment, to understand people, politics,
the atom, God—any object whatsoever. But to make a judgment on any of
these is generally a more serious matter.   Once more, I appeal to my
courtroom paradigm and the role of the jury. That may not be the normal
role of an average citizen but, when it is thrust upon us, with someone's life perhaps hinging on our judgment, would it not be helpful to
know something of what judgment is, and what the conditions of its
rational exercise? Does it not seem in retrospect a pity that, while we
were taught reading, writing, and arithmetic, we were never taught much
on so responsible an activity as judging?   We have come a long way from
trial by ordeal to trial by jury; is no further progress possible? Or
will our descendants look on our failure to teach judgment much as we
look on medieval trial by ordeal?   And perhaps I may remind readers
that, though we may never hold the life of another in the power of our
"Yes" or "No," we do hold in that power, as exercised in daily conversation, the good name of our neighbors, our leaders, our enemies. Is
there not a good case, then, for asking educators to be concerned about
judgment and how it may be taught?

     a. The first factor in judgment, as in understanding, is the
dynamism that is given, built-in, part of our nature. But that dynamism
is a versatile force of universal application; it operates in a new way
when confronted with ideas instead of with data. Before data, the dynamism expressed itself in wonder: what can this be? Now it expresses
itself in reflection: is my idea of what this might be the correct idea?
The same unitary "nature" is at work, the one dynamism, differentiating
itself into the questions appropriate at each level of activity.

     Though such reflection is natural, we will presently take the
position that it can be trained.   As a preliminary, meanwhile, we could
note that there are proverbs that guide judgment and/or decision in
everyday matters: "Look before you leap."   But this will not be ultimately helpful, if only because a smart pupil will immediately think of
an opposing proverb: "He who hesitates is lost." That very opposition,
however, can be turned to profit; the wise teacher will use it to show
the sort of guidance proverbs give: they are incomplete guides to truth,
sometimes but not always applicable, providing checks and balances
rather than definitive reasons. The teacher might then go on to inculcate the basic need if we would judge properly, namely, critical reflec-

tion on the ideas that present themselves. Devices to teach this are
legion: a word on that presently. But the basic precept is single and
simple: reflect. Expanded, it might read: ideas are "a dime a dozen,"
but judgments are sterling silver; reflect before a cheaply bought idea
is given the value of an expensive truth.

b. As the act of reflection is required, so is "material" on
which to reflect. I have spoken of reflection on ideas, but they are
the focus, not the field. Generically, material is supplied by the
preceding activity of consciousness. As earlier for understanding the
"material" object was data become images, so now the object, focused
against the background of images and data, is our set of ideas. The
plural is important. We need to form every possible idea, to think of
all possible explanations, if we are to judge rationally on the correct
one. None is to be excluded in advance. I don't mean that there is no
a priori stand ever to be taken; but it will be taken on the basis of
previous rational judgments. I don't mean that every idea will be worth
serious attention; some are almost immediately seen to be silly. But
the chief point remains. Let ideas occur, let them occur in abundance.
And never, never tell a well-meaning child its idea is silly.[12]

What I have been saying is that reflection is something like a
checking process: the truth is the correct idea, so we have to let idea
challenge idea. Newman's description of a university is relevant here;
let us see it again. What is a university?

> It is the place ... in which the intellect may safely range and
> speculate, sure to find its equal in some antagonist activity,
> and its judge in the tribunal of truth. It is a place where
> inquiry is pushed forward, and discoveries verified and per-

---

12. Note that, besides data and ideas, concepts and their derivatives
enter the field of reflection, for a campaign against conceptualism
is not a campaign against clear thinking. Ideas must be weighed,
and the condition for this is that they be brought to formulation
(conception), defined, expressed in words, so that implications may
be discerned and hypotheses tested. The hasty judgments we
encounter daily and hourly will show this need clearly enough, and
the good teacher will have no trouble meeting the need.

fected, and rashness rendered innocuous, and error exposed, by
the collision of mind with mind, and knowledge with knowledge.[13]

It is a beautiful description of the way of critical reflection, but I
beg to point out one important feature of criticism, one with which
Newman would be in entire agreement: my criticism is to be directed
first against my own ideas; the check I operate is a check on myself.
The current demand for the exercise of criticism, the counterpart of the
demand that the students think for themselves, is often a demand for
criticism of the tradition. Very good; let there be such criticism, let
it flourish. But be sure that the first and last focus of criticism is
your own ideas.

     c. Now what is judgment itself?   What happens in the act of
judging? And how do we know it has happened in the right way? Few
questions are more important for a philosophy of the human, and few more
neglected. But I can name two guides to an answer: Newman in his
detailed study of the act of assent, and Lonergan in his more compact
and technical study of reasonable affirmation.   To note first: we are
not talking now of deduction, of the sort of activity that can be performed by a machine, if we program it properly and feed in materials.
We are talking about concrete matters of fact or perhaps about the
premises we feed into the machine.   Newman's famous example puts the
question whether Great Britain is an island. Of course it is, everyone
knows that. But how do you know?   The person with the ready answer may
soon discover there is more to the question than at first appears.
Newman's own answer to such questions was couched in terms of converging
probabilities.

     It is the cumulation of probabilities, independent of each
     other, arising out of the nature and circumstances of the parti-
     cular case which is under review; probabilities too fine to
     avail separately, too subtle and circuitous to be convertible
     into syllogisms, too numerous and various for such conversion,
     even were they convertible.[14]

_____

13. Newman, Grammar of Assent, p. 377.

14. Newman, Grammar of Assent, p. 288.

Such language, perhaps, is anathema to the logician; it is, however,
crucial for the point at issue, so let us see another long quotation
from Newman:

> It is by the strength, variety, or multiplicity of premisses,
> which are only probable, not by invincible syllogisms,—by
> objections overcome, by adverse theories neutralized, by diffi-
> culties gradually clearing up, by exceptions proving the rule,
> by unlooked-for correlations found with received truths, by
> suspense and delay in the process issuing in triumphant reac-
> tions,—by all these ways, and many others, it is that the
> practised and experienced mind is able to make a sure divination
> that a conclusion is inevitable, of which his lines of reasoning
> do not actually put him in possession.[15]

Lonergan's contribution follows Newman, adding the precision of a
more technical language, and inserting the act of judgment into a more
analytic and, at the same time, more integrated view of human operations. Let me simply state the practical advice that follows from his
position: let the questions occur (reflection); let one's judgment be
exercised in a field where one has achieved some mastery (see Newman's
"practised and experienced mind"); but, because one cannot start there,
let one be willing to learn, (here, all the input of Lonergan's famous
"self-correcting process of learning"); when the evidence is not in and
weighed, let not rashness hurry us to a judgment; when it is in and
weighed, let not temperamental indecision persuade us to shirk the onus
any longer.[16]

     d. The question for educators now becomes the following. If the
nature of judgment and the conditions of its exercise be such as
described, can judgment be taught? Can we form the young student in the
practise of good judgment? A preliminary position on the question was
taken above, but now we have to go into the matter more deeply. For the
question here is not at all the same as the question about teaching
understanding. In one way it seems simpler, for we cannot give under-

---

15. Newman, Grammar of Assent, p. 321.

16. See Lonergan, Insight, especially the section on "Insights into
    Concrete Situations," pp. 283-287—though all of chapters 9 and 10
    will be helpful in grasping this crucial notion.

standing to another; we can only, like Socrates, be a midwife at its
birth. Judgments, on the contrary, can be transferred, in that special
way which is the way of belief; you can tell me that you are tired
listening to me, and I can believe you.   Still, that is not really
teaching judgment; it could become the "banking" concept of education at
its worst. To teach judgment is to foster the interior growth of the
capacity for judging. For that we need, when the question is of education, a certain amount of exercise and practise, and it is just exercise
and practise, in authentic judgments of some significance, that is
difficult; there are so few such judgments that are within the capacity
of the young. Of course, judgments of the "It is raining" type are
myriad, but they will bore the pupil. And, worse, they will foster the
idea that judging is similar to looking out the window, instead of being
a rational act building on a real understanding.

One step toward our goal is to set over against judgment the
activity of debating. As it helped to see the simple type of generalizing as an intermediate step between experience and understanding, so I
propose debating as such a step between understanding and judgment. I
mean debating as it is practised in the schoolroom, where it is known to
be simply "practise," or ought to be so known. Later I will speak,
critically enough, of the debates for keeps that rage in lawcourt and
Parliament. But the question here is of school debates, and my simple
point is that they are not an exercise in truth. This is clear from the
fact that two sides may toss a coin to see which takes the affirmative,
and that it is not a lying act to uphold a position one does not believe
in. Debating then is an exercise on the level of ideas, concerned with
the development, argumentative presentation, and defense of ideas, as
if, but only as if, the idea was coincident with truth. Just as the
Thomist cogitativa did not care about understanding (the practical nurse
does not care why these medicines work, as long as they do), so debating
does not care which side has the truth.   These remarks show us what a
serious matter it is to try to teach judgment, in comparison with
teaching ideas. Not only are ideas "a dime a dozen," that is, quanti-
tatively prolific and so to be had cheaply; they are cheap also in the
quality of the subjective act: they do not commit the one who has them.
Truth is not cheap; the few truths we really possess are acquired
slowly, laboriously, and with a commitment that approaches the sacred.
Our way of teaching judgment must be governed accordingly.

What, then, of exercises in judgment? Naturally, they will be graduated according to the pupil's ability. A first exercise might be one of separating what I know on my own from what I have heard from others—with the latter divided again into what I could check for myself and what I cannot, not conveniently, anyway. We might go on to reflect on erroneous judgments we have made in the past: can I remember once holding a view I later discovered to be wrong? This might lead me to examine my present set of judgments for erroneously accepted beliefs or formed opinions. Then we might be taught a care for getting at the facts in the more everyday type of judgment: "Let's look at the record," as a famous phrase has it.

But mostly the above will be a matter of simple information, to be ascertained by looking up an almanac or consulting eyewitnesses. That is not the kind of judgment on which we most need training and exercise. It is not the kind, generally, that a jury has to make; if it were, there would hardly be a need for a jury. The judgment I have in mind deals with the kind of question that is argued in a debate. In other words, the topic you choose for a debate may be the very topic you choose for an exercise in judgment. But the exercises are worlds apart; in one a battle of wits, in the other the attempt to find the truth. In fact, there might be a great advantage in taking the same topic in sequence, for a debate first, for a judgment second.

Does my proposition seem utterly ludicrous? We would propose quite readily for a class debate such topics as these: Do winter or summer sports do more good for the nation? Is poverty or wealth a more cohesive force in the family? But there is a truth involved in such questions. Why therefore, instead of having two sides debate them, should we not engage the whole class in investigating their truth? Would we feel ill at ease in such a class project? If the supervisor entered, would we timidly pretend we were exercising the class in a debate? I am very much afraid that this would be the normal reaction; if I am right, it is an indication of the need we have as educators to educate ourselves before we can introduce any radical reforms into the education of others.

4. Values and Their Formation

The sequence in what we have called development from below upward, brings us now to the fourth level, that of values, deliberation,
decision, action. This development follows the child's advance in years
(at first, there is lots of experience, little understanding, and almost
no judgment), so we will not expect mature deliberation from the child,
and the values held will be those received from family and community as
a heritage (chapter three). Still, children are quite capable of
receiving such values and of holding firmly to them—one thinks of the
mother of the book of Maccabees and her youngest son (2 Mc 7)—while yet
lacking the experience that might qualify them to lead a nation and
guide its policies. Thus, the diversity of the two ways of development
emerges more clearly than ever at this level, as does their need of one
another and the limitation inherent in discussing them in separate chapters. Once again, I can only ask the reader to consider chapters two to
four as a unit.

a. Our need now is for a grasp of what values are, of the conditions of their formation, of their place and role in the whole process
of human intentional activity—the same sort of need we faced in the
three preceding sections. As before, then, the operator of the whole
process is the built-in dynamism of human consciousness expressing
itself as a capacity, a desire, a need. So the basic precept is still
to respect the dynamism, to give it free rein to operate, to generate
the question proper to each level. What is the question proper to the
fourth level? "What?" and "Why?" brought us to the second level. "Is
it true?" brought us to the third. In the same way we must study the
emergence of the fourth.

We could describe this emergence in contemporary terms by saying
that it adds "ought" or "should" to "is." But then I have to advise
those readers who are trying to enter into the philosophical context
supposed in this book, that they set aside the whole immense effort, on
which reams and reams have been written, to derive "ought" from "is" by
some logical process. In the position adopted here, there is no such

derivation, and it is a waste of time and effort to attempt it. For it
is the dynamism as operational that creates our "ought," just as it is
the dynamism as operational that creates our "is" and our "what." And
just as there is no logical derivation of any "what" or any idea from
any assembly of data, just as there is no logical derivation of any
human "is" from any idea or whatness, so there is none of "ought" from
"is." The whole business goes beyond the derivation of implicit from
explicit content. It is rather the progress of an unfolding dynamism, a
dynamism that studies data to form an idea not given with the data (the
intelligibility immanent in the data is not that of a conclusion in a
premise), that studies ideas to form a factual judgment not given with
the idea (the reference toward being in the idea is that of a possibility of being, not the actuality of "is"), and that studies a factual
situation to form a responsible attitude not given with the situation.
We rely then on the dynamism to do its work in some fashion. If the
dynamism does not operate at all, we are dealing with something less
than human and questions of education do not arise. But, if the dynamism works more or less efficiently, then there is a field for the
educator, on the fourth level as on the others.

Now, because we are prone to let the dynamism lie unnoticed on
the fourth level as on the others, the educator's job is to awaken
advertence to it. For guidelines, I would suggest something like this.
As "What?" and "Why?" are promoted by contrast with an inactive, un-
wondering mind, and as "Is it?" and "Is it not?" are promoted by contrast with a shallow viewiness, partisan stance, and the like, so
"Should I?" and "Should I not?" are promoted by contrast with selfish-
ness and mere satisfaction of selfish desires. For the child learns
early and easily what it is to be selfish; there is an I-Thou in its
life which enables it to see the unworthiness of seeking its own satisfaction in disregard of others (the cake that mother left her two children to divide, and the many stories based on it, will show what I
mean). Another, and very powerful, consideration is that of civic
responsibility. For several years the media have been prodding us on
this matter (stories of citizens passing by on the other side while
someone is stabbed to death, and so on), and it should not be hard for
the teacher to heighten a pupil's consciousness on this level.

b. The narrow views within which the selfish child makes its choices will reveal at once the "materials" on which dynamic conscious-ness should operate in responsible behavior. So will the general rule that the materials are those that have accumulated as a result of prior operations. As the materials for the first advance were found in data, and those for the second in the complex of data, ideas, concepts, impli-cations, surrounding a particular question on a judgment of fact, so the materials now broaden to a still greater sweep; indeed, since we are moving to the existential level, they are as large as life itself. Consider this passage:

> The judgment of value presupposes knowledge of human life, of
> human possibilities proximate and remote, of the probable conse-
> quences of projected courses of action ... But knowledge alone
> is not enough ... moral feelings have to be cultivated. ...
> Finally, [there is] the existential discovery ... that one not
> only chooses ... but also thereby$_{17}$ makes oneself an authentic
> human being or an unauthentic one.

Thus, the field includes the subject and his or her finality, a world of other subjects and their concerns, the whole wide universe in which together they must live out their destiny.   One understands why civil law withholds the vote till the age of twenty-one, or thereabouts, why Aristotle thought it impractical to teach ethics to the young, and why Lonergan makes human development from above downward the prior and more fundamental way of forming the child.

c. Our third question, as on other levels, asks about the actual process of making a decision.   Here, where we have volumes and volumes

---

17. Lonergan, Method, p. 38.   Lonergan's exposition of judgments of value (pp. 36-41) is the source of my exposition of the is-ought question, but his own position on the latter question is too complex to go into fully here.   Clearly, his derivation of 'ought' in Insight was more speculative (see p. 600), and clearly too he retains a sharp distinction in Method between knowing the good and performing it (p. 37). But knowing the good in judgments of value is not merely cognitive, as knowing is in judgments of fact; judgments of value "go beyond merely intentional self-transcendence" and they head "towards moral self-transcendence," though "without reaching the fulness of moral self-transcendence" (p. 37). But this activity of deliberation and conscience is due to the dynamism promoting us from the third level of consciousness to the fourth, and that is sufficient for my point.

from exponents of group dynamics, psychologists, directors in ascetical
practise, and other guides to the conduct of life, I propose to be very
brief. Supposing the positive input that is to be had from all those
educators just listed, and limiting the question to the negative aspect
of the move from deliberating to decision, I will simply propose two
quotations that I find helpful and illuminating. The first is a favorite of mine from Kierkegaard, precisely on the problem of making a
decision (under the general heading of becoming subjective):

> [I]t is assumed that reflection can be halted objectively,
> though the truth is the precise contrary; objectively it is not
> to be stopped, and when it is halted subjectively it does not
> stop itself, but it is the subject who stops it.
>
> Take an example. As soon as Rötscher ... sets himself the task
> of explaining Hamlet, he knows that reflection can be halted
> only by means of a resolve.[18]

The second is from Lonergan, who speaks of deliberation in the very
specific sense that distinguishes it from reflection at the level of
judgment:

> [T]he process of deliberation and evaluation is not itself
> decisive, and so we experience our liberty as the active thrust
> of the subject terminating the process of deliberation by set-
> tling on one of the possible courses of action and proceeding to
> execute it.[19]

     d. Decisions are daily occurrences, but a set of values is the
work of long years. Indeed, the work of a lifetime, for it is a major
component in the business of becoming authentically human. By the same
token it will be a major concern of educators who would train their
pupils in living and not just in making a living. How then can we help
our pupils form a set of authentic values?

     Let us backtrack a moment, and try to put the present question in
perspective. The values that will guide human living suppose a general
knowledge of human nature and human history.   Not so much, at this

---

18. Søren Kierkegaard, Concluding Unscientific Postscript, edited by
    David F. Swenson and Walter Lowrie (Princeton: Princeton University
    Press, 1968), p. 105.

19. Lonergan, Method, p. 50.

stage, the nature that is studied in the human sciences, but the nature
that is revealed in Shakespeare's dramas; and not so much the history
that is a list of rulers and battles and their dates, but the sort we
get in Barbara Tuchman's The Guns of August, where the course of a war
is seen in the context of human folly. Along with such knowledge, and
already to some extent included in it, there is acquired that refinement
of feeling which the higher values presuppose, a refinement that is
learned in the home and carried forward by acquaintance with history,
literature, movies, etc. All this is a way of saying that development
which moves from above downward in the communication of a heritage is
the more important element by far in the early forming of values. But
our heritage is first received in the kind of apprehension that Newman
calls "notional"; to convert it into "real" apprehension we must add our
own experience to the vicarious experience we accumulate in taking
possession of our heritage.[20] The flattery encountered in Aesop's fable
of the fox and the crow is "really" apprehended when I am conned for the
first time by a flatterer among my acquaintances. Here, more clearly
than at any other level, we see the complementarity of development from
below with that from above. If my tactics require me to postpone discussion of the latter till the next chapter, the former has to be taken
up now. How then can the pupil's experience, developing in life with
siblings, parents, schoolmates, neighbors, the village community, how
can it be used to convert "notional" apprehension of values into "real"
apprehension? More generally, how can the educator assist the pupil in
the formation of personally achieved values?

My own first piece of advice would be a warning: beware of
leading the young too swiftly or too seriously along the path of decision. I do not mean simply that we should let children be children,
and not impose adult burdens on childish shoulders; that also is wise:
fun and games belong to youth, and care and concern to later years. But
I am thinking of a built-in limitation in training others for responsibility, in "practising" decisions. I mean that one can practise experiencing: one has just to open one's eyes and look. One can practise
understanding: one will find a book of problems and try to solve them.
One can practise a bit of the art and learn a bit of the wisdom of

20. Newman, Grammar of Assent, passim but especially the first four
    chapters. We shall return to this topic in chapter four here.

judgment: there are types of "exercise" judgments to make that will not
seriously affect the course of my life or form in a significant way my
character. But one cannot "practise" making decisions; if it is mere
practise, it will not be a real decision. If it is a real decision, it
will not be mere practise, but a real factor in making me what I am.
And the latter is too serious a business to be "practised" in the classroom without infinite caution.

Let me expand this important point. The highest function of
these four levels is for me to take hold of my life, to decide what I am
going to make of myself. And this is a decision of enormous import. As
Lonergan says of our choices and actions, in them we have "the work of
the free and responsible subject producing the first and only edition of
himself."[21] It is a matter then in which there may be need of the
involvement of school, church, counselor, and parent with the pupil.
Not to make all his or her decisions, but to assist the first fumbling
steps in decision, to guide gently the gradual course of the decision,
to head off decisions that might hang an albatross around the pupil's
neck for life, but at the same time to allow the freedom to make mistakes in minor matters, in the hope that lesser mistakes made earlier
may help prevent more serious and even disastrous mistakes later.

With all that said by way of preface and precaution, we have
still to talk of positive exercises. Let us separate the question as it
pertains to value judgments, from the question of existential decisions
in which the pupil achieves full moral self-transcendence. Training for
value judgments will take the early form of creating ideals, ideals that
the pupil may already have received from tradition, in a notional apprehension unrelated to life, but ideals that have now to be immanently
generated and really apprehended. Exercises here do not present such a
serious problem to the educator. They can indeed be a direct continu-
ation of the earlier exercises in forming judgments; only now the effort
will be to form judgments on moral matters. And one can perhaps keep
these questions from becoming matter for existential decision (if that
step seems premature for particular pupils) by trying to work out the
ideal in a more general form. For example, not raising the question of
the spring seal-hunt, but rather the question of our attitude toward

---

21. In the lecture on "The Subject," Lonergan, <u>A Second Collection</u>, p.
    83.

animals in general; not the question of Quebec separatism, but that of
the rights in general of groups within groups.

But we have finally to discuss the business of decisions themselves. First, notice that there is material at hand. That is, the
child, and much more the youth, will have been making decisions more and
more frequently. What "use" can be made of this fact in education?
Perhaps the pupil can be helped to reflect on what has been decided, to
analyze the decision, to see what elements go into a proper decision, to
correct omissions, etc. But I am inclined to think it possible also for
a class to engage once in a while in a really value-forming existential
choice, even as a class. Let me illustrate by an example from my own
long ago school days. It was the custom for each class graduating from
high school to be represented by a great wooden shield, which would bear
the class motto and be hung in the assembly hall. Our motto, I think,
was "Carpe diem." As far as I can remember, the choice of the motto was
not an existential exercise for the class.   But why should it not be?
Why should not the class, early in the year, discuss and form a really
personal value judgment on the ideal represented in the motto? Why
should not each member—individually, of course, but how much more
firmly through community support—decide to make that motto part of his
or her own life? As I was writing these paragraphs, a newscast showed
us a class of pupils (in the seventh grade, if I remember rightly), who
had made a movie to portray the courage of one of their town who is a
national hero, Terry Fox. Their achievement makes the project I suggest
quite pedestrian by contrast, but the point of each could be the same.

There is surely no lack of such ideals, such mottoes, such
projects, no lack of worthy causes adrift in the world. Are we missing
out in our training of youth by not utilizing more of them? I do not
belittle the "corporal works of mercy" that our students perform:
Christmas parcels for the poor, and so on. I only say that there should
be in such works, a true creation of values, immanently generated
through the long pondering that forms one's ideals; there should be also
the careful deliberation that ensures one's real involvement. This is
the sort of thing a school might cautiously promote. Of course, religious training would have long been doing its bit: "Quid hoc ad aeterni-
tatem?" And so on. And no doubt secondary education could close with
what we call in Catholic circles, a retreat of election. But now we are
coming to the choice of a career and I think that kind of consideration
belongs in another chapter.

5. Conclusions and Reflections

By now the role I gave our courtroom scene in chapter one may be
clearer: that of providing a defined structure for the basic human activities, and therefore a framework to help educators help the child, the
pupil, the youth, to grow and achieve according to the built-in poten-
tialities of human nature.   Of course, the deficiencies of the model
will also be clearer. For one thing, the pupil is not four persons, one
assembling data, another offering an explanation, a third judging the
truth of the matter, and a fourth taking action—with all four standing
in relation to one who may intervene at the higher level of mercy and
love. The pupil is one person doing all these things together, without
distinguishing them until perhaps a particular case, or a Socratic
teacher, brings the pupil to realize the differences, to realize that to
collect data is not to have understanding, to have ideas is not to have
judgment, etc. Again, the pupil does not function in the setting of a
legal system established for one purpose, and that purpose focused on a
very particular fact-finding task which is by no means the whole of
life. Pupils are alive with the exuberance of the young. Their experience ranges at will from outer to inner, from factual to fantastic.
Where fantasy might be excluded from a courtroom, it is one of the
pupil's most precious capacities.   Where judgment and decision are the
immediate goal of the courtroom, they are only a distant responsibility
while the child is young. Still, the pattern is there, more compact by
far in the child than in the proceedings of the courtroom; it would be
odd if it had no relevance to education.

To speak of the four levels and their basic activities as the
"constants" of human development is, of course, to acknowledge tacitly a
whole world of variable factors that have not entered these pages. Let
me, for the sake of perspective, take an example from that world. A
friend of mine, for many years now a missionary in India and much concerned about the poor children there who cannot afford an education,
developed in his school a Poultry Project which 150 boys, working a
couple of hours a day, could run from A to Z, and thereby pay for their
education. The financial side is especially important in India. What
is important to all educators is the work-centered idea of education.

These boys, from fifth to tenth grade, in the context of caring for their "poultry farm" and marketing its products, learn carpentry and electrical work, accounting and mathematics, a fair amount of physics, chemistry and biology in a living laboratory, a certain amount even of such subjects as civics and economics.   They learn to use a library to study the specialized literature on their project. Maybe most important of all, they learn cooperation, develop a community spirit, and form habits for life.[22]   While I believe, then, that experience, under-standing, reflection, and values are constants in education, whether the locus be an Ivy League university or a poor district of Darjeeling, India, it is also true that they refer to operations, operations are impossible without materials, and how infinitely preferable are real-life materials to those concocted in the teacher's imagination. One of the few dreary memories of my boyhood schooldays is that of working on endless problems about laying carpets with patterns of certain sizes in rooms of certain sizes—a subject about which I could hardly care less.

May this one example stand for the hundreds and hundreds of topics that pertain to education, questions of books and curricula, of machines and methods, of plant and personnel, of parent-teacher co-operation and of extra-curricular activities of the pupil—the list has no end. The more books I read on the matter, the better I realize how futile, and unnecessary, it would be for me to try to become a crash-course expert in so demanding a field of specialization. I have to be content to make my little contribution under the heading of educational constants: experience, understanding, reflection, and values as struc-turing the way of achievement.

But the constants in education belong to us as human, which means that they belong in the teacher as well as in the pupil. And that brings up a factor in education that I have mentioned only casually, though it is most important of all after the pupil: the role of the teacher. This is twofold: to assist the pupil in the way of achieve-ment, but to be guide, philosopher, and friend in the way of heritage,

---

22. See J. M. Abraham, "SAS Poultry: Eggs and Education," Indian Poultry
    Review, V, 2 (Sept. 1, 1973), pp. 127-135 ("SAS" stands for "Saint
    Alphonsus School").

contributing from the fulness of his or her own development on the four
levels to a corresponding development in the young. This role will come
more into focus in the next two chapters.

CHAPTER THREE

EDUCATION AS HERITAGE

With all their good will, and their resolve to reserve judgment
till after chapter four, readers must have found the previous chapter a
bit like clapping with one hand.   It was so obviously deficient as a
view of education. One might indeed simply point to the deficiencies in
the way of achievement, in order to justify the complementary path of
development from above downward, along which the human comes to the
child as heritage, faithfully preserved and responsibly handed on
(traditum) by parent, teacher, church, society, and received in trust by
child and pupil, with acceptance of the role of heir to a community
patrimony. But the way of heritage has its own independent justifica-
tion, put as follows in an ancient saying that has become proverbial:

> We are like dwarfs sitting on the shoulders of giants; we see
> more things, and more far-off ones, than they did, not because
> our sight is better, nor because we are taller than they were,
> but because they raise us up and add to our height by their
> gigantic loftiness.[1]

Such sentiments are anathema to extremists on the progressive side, and
even traditionalists will find excessive such veneration for the past.
But the quotation does make an obviously valid, if very trite point,
namely, we owe a great debt to the past; and so it will serve to introduce this chapter, which belongs to tradition, or to the human received
as gift by the child, or to education as handing on a heritage.
    The "obviously valid point" in the proverb of dwarfs on giants'
shoulders happens nowadays to be disputed, so we had better delay a bit
on the obvious. Still, there is no need to prolong the delay. The

---

1. Quoted in Etienne Gilson, History of Christian Philosophy in the
   Middle Ages (New York: Random House, 1955), p. 619. It occurs in
   John of Salisbury, Metalogicon, III, 4, who attributes it to Bernard
   of Chartres (died between 1124 and 1130; see Gilson, p. 140).

opposite position, in its extreme formulation, is simply self-destructive. To say, for example, that it is not at all the business of education to transmit values, ideals, judgments, to the young, but rather to
teach them to think for themselves, to make their own judgments and
decisions, and thus to progress from sandbox to nuclear laboratory, is
already to have transmitted to pupils a multitude of judgments and
values that they did not generate out of their own experience, including
the very basic judgment that this is the way they should be educated,
and the very strategic decision to provide this kind of school for them.
Meeting such a self-destructive contradiction at the start, we feel less
inclined to delay on the further questions that arise; for example, the
question how much the enemies of tradition relied on what they themselves received from tradition to be able to make this judgment and
decision for the next generation; or, what our hope is, if a child be
left to develop freely in the sandbox, that a nuclear scientist and not
just a goon, will eventually emerge; or, why we should be skeptical of
all positions advocated in the past, and this on the urging of those who
advocate such vandalism without a trace of skepticism with regard to
their own position.

     The reader will detect a certain sarcasm in these remarks, and
may suspect a bias on my part in favor of tradition. It is true that I
give the priority to tradition, and true that I regard a good deal of
the present iconoclasm in education as simple vandalism; but whether
those judgments are biased, or true and verifiable, remains to be seen.
Two things, however, may be conceded at once. One, that it is only the
extremist position that is self-destructive; still, it is good to have
seen how self-destructive it is, good to realize that I cannot say, "All
positions are to be abandoned," without adding as an afterthought,
"except the one I just took." The other: this is a time of great and
rapid change, and many bastions of tradition are falling, and the rest
are subject to criticism. But that only makes it the more urgent to get
down to bedrock and find the constants that really are constant in human
development. I have declared my set of constants, and tried to show in
chapter two how they might lead a child, not without guidance, from
sandbox to nuclear science. The same constants obtain in the way of
heritage—naturally so, else they would not be constants. But, naturally also, they function somewhat differently here.

It is in the nature of tradition to grow, like Topsy, in a rather disorganized way. It is in the nature of handing on tradition that it be a fact long before it be a theme of discussion. This was true also of development from below upward, but with the difference there that the operators of the development were internal to the pupils' consciousness, and subject therefore to a greater measure of control on their part than in the handing on of tradition. In any case, there is a measure of obscurity and difficulty in trying to set forth the way of heritage, so I propose a somewhat different method from that used in chapter two.[2] I will not begin by setting forth the sequence of steps according to the clear pattern of the four levels of consciousness, but will first take a paradigm case of a child growing into adolescence in a particular educational system, and see what sorts of things happen there. On that basis, I will go on, in a second section, to relate the data collected to that structure of consciousness that we have found to be built into human nature. What I am saying is that the skeletal structure of experience, understanding, reflection, and values, can be more clearly seen to obtain in the lawcourt and in the child's spontaneous development along the path of personal achievement. I believe the same structure still obtains, and that the analysis of chapter two will help us discover it, in the way of heritage. But I freely admit that the skeleton is not so obviously discernible; hence, my rather roundabout approach. — One more preliminary note: my paradigm case is not contemporary, but one familiar to me, namely, the type of school program I knew sixty years ago. But, if the constants are really constant, that will not matter much.

1. A Paradigm: The Ontario Schools of the 1920s

My paradigm case will be the Ontario school system of the 1920s, chosen because it is available for study in the city where I write, and similar enough to the system of my own schooldays in New Brunswick to make it a ready source for the recall of memories and long gone experi-

---

2. For the upward path from experience through understanding and judgment to values we have the detailed work of a lifetime in Lonergan's writings; we lack that guidance for the downward path.

ences. It is very much the system of United Empire Loyalists, with
their values, their biases, their judgments on history. But, if values
and judgments are communicated by much the same methods, whether the
system be that of Scottish Calvinists, Irish Catholics, Daughters of the
American Revolution, Quebec Separatists, then the particularities of the
paradigm will not matter much.   It may matter somewhat more that the
system worked on me as a Catholic boy of Irish ancestry, that it belongs
to the rural scene symbolized by Gray's "Elegy Written in a Country
Church-yard" and the like, but such details will not present a major
problem. There may even be an advantage that the heritage was received
by a somewhat alien subject, that it is presented now in times so
different, for perhaps we can examine it more objectively as a consequence. It would be unwise, for example, to use the Canadian Catechism
as a paradigm; much as that project promises for better catechetics, it
is so controverted that the paradigmatic element would likely be lost in
the sound and fury. No one is likely to argue with the same involvement
now about the Ontario system of the early part of the century.

     Within that system   I will focus on the books we called
"Readers"—little anthologies of prose and poetry by which various
language skills were taught, and, as well (this is my main point and
contention), values and judgments were handed on to the pupil. The
Readers, to be sure, were only part of the system. Arithmetic and
algebra contributed something too, even to values; much more did history, and a set of "Health Readers" which bore down on the twin evils of
smoking and drinking. Then the school system itself was only part of
the larger system comprised of school and home, of chums and community,
of church and country. But the prose and poetry Readers of school will
provide plenty of data for present purposes.[3]

     I begin with a book published in 1920, authorized by the Ontario
Ministry of Education, and called simply Primer. Internal evidence
shows it was intended for seven-year-olds, who presumably had already

3. I express here my gratitude to the librarians in the archives section
   of The Ontario Institute for Studies in Education, Toronto, where I
   collected much of the material for this chapter. Later I was able to
   consult also the collection of school textbooks in the Harriet Irving
   Library of the University of New Brunswick, Fredericton; my thanks to
   the librarians of that institution as well.

learned the alphabet and a few simple words. It begins with the familiar story of the little red hen. Who will help me plant the grain? she asked. Not I, from cat and dog and pig. Then I will do it, she said. Similarly, with the next question, Who will help me cut the grain? The same answer from all three, and so the little red hen did it herself. Thus, through the stages of grinding the grain, and baking the cake. After several pages (Primers don't have much on a page) comes the peripeteia, Who will help me eat the cake? I will, said cat and dog and pig. No, you won't, said the little red hen; you would not plant or cut or grind or bake; you will not eat either.

My question now is this: what is happening here from the viewpoint of our twofold way of development? That is, what is happening over and above the training in spelling, grammar, and other skills? Most surely, there is a transfer of morality, in the sense of moral judgment and moral ideals, from system and teacher to pupil. Like the medieval morality plays, the piece would teach virtue, in this case, inculcate the virtue of industry, the principle that rewards belong to those who earn them; perhaps there is evidence also of a religious ethic congenial to certain denominations of the church. The point now is not to discuss the values communicated, but simply to note that they are communicated, and this through the medium of a story.

Such is the intention of the giver, of those who drew up the school system, and of the teacher who goes along with the system. But what of the child? On what basis does he or she receive the value, the morality, the ideal? I presume children do receive it, if no one is born a rebel, for few would have the habit of rebellion so formed at seven as to challenge "what the book says." Most surely again, they receive it in an attitude of implicit trust—trust in parents and teacher, in the school system, in the universe in general. To begin with the latter, which is really very fundamental, there is, I think, a kind of natural peace, harmony, conformity, that the child spontaneously feels toward the universe, the world of being, of what is. So I have argued elsewhere, partly from the nature of mind and heart and soul in the child, partly from the observable phenomena of children, their delight in what is during those innocent years before they acquire the cares of adults.[4] Just to hear this _Primer_ story would, in that case, dispose the child to accept its lessons. Add to that, the fact that parents send the child to school and attach great importance to its learning what is given there, and we will certainly not expect the child to challenge the lesson. Finally, there are the teachers themselves, and what they communicate to the child through their attitude to this story. To that we will return, for it is the heart of the way of tradition.

So far, the obvious. Questions spring to mind, of course, whose answers are not at all obvious, but let us postpone them till we have a broader base in factual data for a critique. The _Primer_ then continues with more morality stories—"The Dog in the Manger," "The Greedy Man" (to get rich faster he killed the goose that was laying golden eggs). Of this trend, we hardly need further specimens, though it is worth noticing that little rhymes and not just stories are a vehicle for much worthy advice:

> One thing at a time
> And that done well
> Is the best of all rules
> As many can tell.

More important is a quite different category, represented first by nursery rhymes ("Humpty Dumpty," "Little Jack Horner," "Jack and Jill," and so on) and later by such poetry as Christina Rosetti's "Who Has Seen the Wind?"

> Who has seen the wind?
> Neither I nor you.
> But when the leaves hang trembling,
> The wind is passing through.

---

4. See my articles on "Complacency and Concern in the Thought of St. Thomas," _Theological Studies_ 20 (1959) 1-39, 198-230, 343-395, especially pp. 369-372.

> Who has seen the wind?
> Neither you nor I.
> But when the trees bow down their heads,
> The wind is passing by.

How difficult it is, especially for those now in their old age, when the
first experience of these rhymes has receded into the far distant past—
how difficult it is for us to recapture that experience or even to state
in abstract words what it meant for us.   I put it as simply as I can
when I say that it was the liberation of that precious capacity which we
call fantasy:

> When I was a beggarly boy
> And lived in a cellar damp
> I had not a friend nor a toy
> But I had Aladdin's lamp.

The Primer was the Aladdin's lamp for many a child, or maybe nursery
rhymes had already released his or her fantasy.   Somewhere in those
early years, imagination takes wing and leaves the familiar world of
crib blankets and bottles and toys, and begins to explore the infinite
world of the possible. There is no morality involved here, like that in
the story of "The Little Red Hen."   There is no relation to actual history; if the nursery rhyme was originally a comment on historical
events, that is now forgotten and may well remain forgotten till the
pupil has to write a doctoral dissertation on the topic. Again, if the
child's world of the "possible" is not concretely possible, that too is
a lesson we may leave to later years.   For the time being, the child's
new world is a world of sheer delight.

It is not delight without meaning, as will perhaps appear more
clearly if we take for our study a poem like "Who Has Seen the Wind?"
It does more than liberate fantasy, and delight the imagination; it is
art of a higher genre. Lonergan, in Insight, speaks of art as "a twofold freedom. As it liberates experience from the drag of biological
purposiveness, so it liberates intelligence from the wearying con-
straints of ... proofs ... and ... factualness.   For the validation of

the artistic idea is the artistic deed."[5]   True, art may become symbolic, that is (in Lonergan's use at this point), refer to "an ulterior
purpose or significance," raise questions on humanity and offer answers,
"but, in its subtler forms, it is content to communicate any of the
moods in which such questions arise, to convey any of the tones in which
they may be answered or ignored."[6]

What we encounter here, over and above the world of morality, is
the world of beauty, which is a value in itself, a most precious gift
from one generation to another. And here I must pause to ask a more
critical question. Are there really theorists in the field of education
who would deprive the child of such treasures? Surely there cannot be.
Surely the extremist enemies of tradition have not really thought their
position through in its full implications. For here we are witnessing
"tradition" in a most elementary yet most precious form, the handing on
from generation to generation of the treasures of the past, the accumulated patrimony which is the child's right by inheritance. How many
generations passed before it was possible to write "Who Has Seen the
Wind?" and how would it be possible at all, unless one generation handed
on to the next the refinement of feelings, the cultivation of imagination, that it had itself inherited, and carried further for transmission
to the next generation? And what of opposition to the despised banking
concept of education? Is it not demolished by this one simple example?
Are there not treasures that should be banked in the child's mind, the
earlier the better, so that they will remain in old age to be relived
when, like Wordsworth's daffodils, they

> flash upon that inward eye
> Which is the bliss of solitude?

Banking, of course, is not the right metaphor; we should think rather of
the child's own museum of art, literature, music—its own private store
of treasures.

---

5. Lonergan, Insight, p. 185.

6. Lonergan, Insight, p. 185; for a more detailed treatment, see his
   Method in Theology, pp. 61-64.

It must be, it has to be, that the extremists do not mean what they seem, in perhaps careless moments, to say. If they do not, then we wish to know how they would qualify their positions, and a host of other questions come up. Again, I postpone them till we collect more data from our paradigm. Leaving the Primer, I hasten through other books on the program, able to do so because the values and judgments handed on show a continuity with those in the Primer. There is moralizing verse:

> Little drops of water
> Little grains of sand
> Make the mighty ocean
> And the pleasant land.
> Little deeds of kindness
> Little words of love
> Make our earth an Eden
> Like the Heaven above.

There is moralizing prose, as in Aesop's fables ("The Hare and the Tortoise"). Fantasy moves from a more passive to a more active role:

> When at home alone I sit
> And am very tired of it
> I have just to shut my eyes
> To go sailing through the skies

—where there is a kind of invitation to the pupil to do likewise.

Of course, the scale is graduated. For example, courtesy in a form hardly possible to the seven-year-old pupil is inculcated in the poem about the lad who left his boisterous companions to help an old lady across the street: "She's somebody's mother, boys, you know." There is some attention to the formation of judgment: a welcome note, in view of my critique in chapter two. For example, the story of "The Blind Men and the Elephant" shows how very different views of what an elephant is, can be based on a partial attention to the data. It is almost made to order as an exercise in judgment: collecting all the data, examining all the ideas, reflecting till one finds the correct hypothesis.

But there is no need to add detail to tedious detail. Let me
just note two examples of somewhat special significance before I go on
to more analytic reflection. The first is the gradual inculcation of
the virtues of war. I will not call it militarism, for "ism" suggests a
philosophy, and what we are dealing with is simply a special case of
patriotic partisanship. There is in The First Book (which follows the
Primer) a piece about the brave little girl lighting the beacon when her
father, the lighthouse keeper, was caught in the storm. Nothing military about that, but The Second Reader advances, with a piece of history
about the young hero, Jack Cornwell, who stood at his post on the
Chester during the Battle of Jutland, and died there in defense of his
country. With the Third and Fourth Books there is a great expansion in
the number of war pieces: "The Burial of Sir John Moore," "The Charge of
the Light Brigade," and so on.

To assess this phenomenon you should remember that the Great War
(now redesignated World War I), that tragedy of inhuman carnage, was
just over, not over long enough for much reflection on the awful sense-
lessness of it all. You should know also that there was in Ontario,
dominated then by the United Empire Loyalists, an almost fanatical
devotion to the mother country. What more reasonable, so natural as
almost to escape a deliberate decision, than to form in the impression-
able ten-year-old schoolboy or girl, a similar devotion? I would not
exaggerate. There is an evident will to include Canadian pieces too,
like the Heroine of Verchères. And likewise to widen the base to the
measure of humanity, with stories of the Greeks at Troy, of William Tell
and his son, of "A Roman's Honour," and so on. But England obviously
dominates. The Fourth Book opens with selections from Kipling,
Tennyson, George Eliot, and Shakespeare, followed soon by Robert Louis
Stevenson, Robert Browning, Edmund Gosse, Dickens, and the like. I have
hinted at the difficulties this would make for a Roman Catholic boy or
girl of Irish ancestry; but the point at present is, first, the intent
of the system, which was to foster a patriotic devotion to England, and,
next, the efficacy of the system: what boy or girl could fail to be
moved by such selections,

> The meteor flag of England
> Shall yet terrific burn ...

or, "Nobly, nobly Cape Saint Vincent to the North-West died away"? I think my American friends, and it is they with whom I am most in contact outside my own country, have very little idea of the sort of schooling my generation of Canadians received, and are consequently puzzled that we do not always share their views on international matters.

My other example is not entirely new, for it is continuous with the theme introduced in our very first piece by our now much overworked "Little Red Hen." But there is a new angle, religious at least in this sense that the virtues inculcated are most congenial to a particular denomination. I speak of what we call, rightly or wrongly (the matter is debated), the Protestant work ethic, as practised notably by Swiss and Scottish Calvinists. It is pervasive in the school books of Ontario and New Brunswick of sixty years ago. There is background for it in the stress on honesty of The First Book. We have, for example, the story of the woodsman whose axe, his very livelihood, fell in the river. Mercury came to the rescue, dived and brought up a gold axe, only to hear, No, that's not mine. Similarly with a silver axe. When Mercury, on his third dive, brought up an iron axe and the woodsman claimed it, he was rewarded for his honesty by receiving all three axes. I speak of stress on honesty as "background," for I would not maintain that honesty is exclusively a Calvinist virtue. No doubt, stress in precept and theory on one virtue means ipso facto a lesser attention to other virtues, but that does not mean a lesser degree of virtue in practise; as we might learn from St. Thomas Aquinas, the virtues hang together.

But there are refinements in this ethic that are not quite so incontestable. I turn here to some selections I remember from my own New Brunswick Readers, not found, I think, in those of Ontario. Gems like the following from Isaac Watts:

> How doth the little busy bee
>   Improve each shining hour,
> And gather honey all the day
>   From every opening flower!

Or the piece that is for me the symbol and epitome of this ethic, called simply "Procrastination." As I remember it, a farmer had finished his business in town and decided to call on his lawyer for advice. "Advice?" the lawyer asked. "Advice on what?"—"Just advice."—"Oh."

So the lawyer thought a moment, scribbled something on a bit of paper, and handed it over. The farmer paid his fee and dropped the paper without examination into his pocket.

Arrived home, tired, with his boots off and a drink in his hand (water, surely, or buttermilk, for these were temperance days in New Brunswick), he remembered his "advice" and took it out of his pocket. It read: "Never put off till tomorrow what you can do today." Voilà. On with the boots, out into the fields of cocked hay. By nightfall the hay was safely stored in the barns, much to the farmer's advantage when the floods came and washed away the hay of his procrastinating neighbors— who were perhaps Irish. This, I say, is a symbol for me of the ethic inculcated in our school books. But it became a symbol, and I realized its power, only on the day, long after, when I broke away from it, when I came to realize how much is to be said on the other side for what I call, with due apologies to my Irish ancestors, the Irish Catholic ethic: "Always put off till tomorrow what you don't have to do today."

2. The Pattern of the Paradigm:
Development from Above Downward

Thomist ontology distinguishes a whatness, which it calls the essence of things, from a whyness or howness, which it calls the formal cause, that which makes a thing to be what it is. But it is one and the same intelligibility that we find in essence and formal cause, so the what-question is the same as the why-question. Thus, "to take Aristotle's stock example, 'What is an eclipse of the moon?' and 'Why is the moon thus darkened?' are, not two questions, but one and the same." Still, there is a complexity involved in turning a what-question into a why-question, as when we ask, What is a man? What is a house? "The meaning is, Why is this sort of body a man? Why are stones and bricks arranged in a certain way, a house?" To Scholastics the particular answers are, respectively, the human soul of man, and the artificial form of a house. And one can generalize: "That which makes matter, in general, to be a thing, is the causa essendi, the formal cause."[7]

This little foray into Scholastic metaphysics and cognitional

---

7. Lonergan, Verbum, pp. 12-13, 15.

theory illuminates, for those who will accept it, what I am trying to do. My argument has, as it were, a whatness and a howness. In essence it is an argument for the complementarity of the way of achievement and the way of heritage. But the trick lies in showing how they are complementary, and this howness is explained by the structured unity of human consciousness, the communication between levels, and the possibility of movement in the downward direction of tradition as well as in the upward direction of achievement. It is the pattern of that downward movement that concerns us now. The first section of this chapter gave a rough description of the paradigm case, but the need is for a precise account of the pattern followed.

First, then, there is a dynamism at work, effecting the development from above. Just as the upward development was powered by the capacity for and the drive toward intelligibility, truth, and the good, so the downward development is powered by the love and responsibility of the educator for the child, and the corresponding love for, and ensuing trust in, the educator on the part of the child. This form of communication begins and ends, is given and received, in love.

But now we must broaden the concept of love that served us in chapter one, that existing between parent and child. Lonergan speaks regularly, and helpfully, of three forms of love: the love we have for God in religion, and this is unrestricted, unconditional, total; the love of family members for one another, or domestic love; and the love and loyalty of citizens for their country, which can be extended to include the love of anyone in the human family for the community of men and women who constitute our race.

In this third case, it may seem that the element of reciprocity is lacking; we may love our country, we may love humanity, but how, pray, does country or humanity love us? But perhaps reflection will reveal that this love too, in its own way, is reciprocal. For example, a Queen may love her subjects, and she represents the country in this as in other functions; and, if it seems rather farfetched to speak of President or Prime Minister holding in affection the people they represent, is that not a censure of the Presidents and Prime Ministers we happen to know best? Similarly, we may focus our love for the human race in a Mahatma Ghandi or a Mother Teresa, and they in turn will represent the human race in their love for us.

Leaving aside for a time the love that belongs to religion (see chapter six and the appendix), we will attend more to the other forms, and we will ask how the dynamism of this love effects human development, what paths it follows in human consciousness in the course of conveying the human heritage from generation to generation. We are talking of the patrimony which parents in the family, adult citizens in the community, leaders in the nation, humanitarians in the world confederacy, hold in trust from a preceding generation and hand on in fidelity to the next. Outwardly, it finds verbal expression in prose and poetry, in accounts of history, in mottoes and precepts; but it is embodied also in customs, ceremonies, flags, rituals, parades, jubilee celebrations, and the like. And the most effective expression is not necessarily the most explicitly formulated; we know the saying, Let me write a nation's songs and I care not who may write her laws. But our question regards more directly the internal paths of consciousness. Can we find values communicated and received in loyalty? Can we find judgments based on values received in this way? Can we find understanding of true judgments growing as experience is added to give them a material basis? I think we can, though the stages will not appear with the sharper delineation of our lawcourt scheme, and the evidence will be only such as to fit comfortably into a pattern already established rather than to establish it independently.

On the first step, the communication of values, perhaps our first chapter has said most of what needs to be said. To quote again a key axiom on this matter, "Values are caught ... more than taught." It is comparatively easy to find evidence in more formal education to support that found in home and family. I am thinking of the sort of evidence summed up in the saying that the battle of Waterloo was won on the playing fields of Eton. What does that mean, analyzed and generalized? It means that the character of the English officer, corresponding to what the Romans called virtutes, was formed by his public school tradition, in particular, by the tradition of games ("Play up! Play up! And play the game!"). It means that a system of values was communicated in this tradition—honor before self-satisfaction:

I could not love thee, Dear, so much,
Loved I not Honour more.

Calm discipline when the ranks are breaking:

> If you can keep your head when all about you
> Are losing theirs and blaming it on you ...

and so on.

It is the second step, from values to judgments, that comes more into focus in formal education, so much concerned with the business of knowledge. It is worth noting, to begin with, that our position has the support of two great thinkers, different as they are from one another in many respects. One is Pascal, with his remark now familiar to everyone, that the heart has reasons which reason does not know.[8] The other, the reader may be surprised to learn, is Thomas Aquinas, whose judicium per connaturalitatem, seems to be Pascal's point anticipated by some four centuries.[9]

Pascal and Aquinas would be worth a special study under this heading, but this is not the place for it. I return rather to the English people and their colonial history for evidence that is closer to the everyday scene. It is said[10] that, in the heyday of colonial rule, when communication with the mother country was a matter of letters once or maybe twice a year, there was no possibility of centralized control in the contemporary sense; nor indeed, and the point lies here, was there any need for such minute direction from the top. The character formed in the home, in the schools, in the national tradition, was such as to provide governors who would know, without formal orders, what to do in the situations that might arise in far-off dominions. We have a phrase that says they would know "instinctively," but that language is alien to the philosophy underlying this book; I prefer then to say that their value system enabled them to weigh political and administrative options, and provided for them a criterion of consequent judgment. One

---

8. For Lonergan's understanding of Pascal, see Method, p. 115.

9. Summa theologiae, II-II, q. 45, a. 2.

10. The remark is Lonergan's, in The Philosophy of Education, which I have referred to in the Preface above. In the Quinn transcript, see pp. 129-130.

remembers here, in illustration, the analogous case of the three
brothers in P. C. Wren's novel, Beau Geste: all three, and each in an
individual decision, came to the same conclusion on what should be done
in the situation they faced, namely, assume responsibility for the theft
of their aunt's jewels; not only that, but all took flight along the
same route, ending up together in the French Foreign Legion. A piece of
farfetched fiction, which proves nothing for our case, though it illustrates brilliantly, if rather sadly in the end, the concept I am setting
forth.

Let the reader not be distracted by the feelings my examples may
arouse. The point is not to justify the English colonial policy of a
century ago, or to gloss over its mistakes, or excuse its injustices, or
even to admire its successes. The point is simply to see how it worked,
insofar as it worked; and I think the evidence is that, by and large, it
worked along the lines I have drawn, where loyalty receives a tradition,
the tradition forms a set of ideals and values, and the values direct
judgments and policies of action. Perhaps we may say even more: that it
worked rather better for a mother country which had a tradition without
its codification, than it did for other countries where the codification
might be worked out with academic excellence but a corresponding tradition had not formed. The difficulties of the latter way are illustrated
in my own country, where for fifty years we have struggled, without an
urgently impelling cause, but rationally in the way of achievement, to
work out a constitution for ourselves. By contrast, the United States
of America began with a war of independence that united the thirteen
colonies in a powerful allegiance to a common cause, and the constitution followed with comparative rapidity. And, to take a quite
different field for illustration, Marxism, if I have been correctly
informed about it, combines a deepseated hatred of injustice with a
dogged attempt to analyze the situation of the workers. If that is so,
it provides a remarkable instance of a dynamism from above (love/hatred)
meeting one from below (data, analysis, action) to produce a movement of
extraordinary momentum. But surely it is the love of humanity, the
hatred of injustice, that provides that momentum, rather than the
rational analysis, even if there can be no security in the cause without
correct analysis of the situation.

My chief example, the English tradition as operative in a
colonial setting, was itself too narrow to do more than illustrate the

general lines of the loyalty-values-judgments sequence as seen in a
particular case. But we do not educate our children, nor did the
English for that matter, to prepare them for colonial rule. And so we
must raise the question in general, of what tradition, what values and
judgments, we wish to communicate to the young of the nation in our
schools and to new generations of our human race in the accumulating
tradition of the global village. The human, of course, will be the all-
pervasive category, since patriotism itself is a human virtue, even when
its object differs so much on opposing sides of the battle-line. So the
values and judgments to be communicated will be basically humanitarian,
whether the focus be on the family, or on the nation. The stories that
come to mind from my schoolbooks are those of William Tell, of Blossom
Owens pleading for the life of her brother before Abraham Lincoln, of
Joseph and his brothers in Egypt. In each case there is a family
interest and a national interest, but in all there is likewise a human
interest. The broad category, then, will be human nature: not human
nature as a sociologist might conceive it, but as an artist does, human
nature alive in particular people. And the values and judgments will be
those learned in stories and poetry on how people behave, on what they
are like, what their weaknesses, what their possibilities of greatness.
And the general lessons will be on living with people and dealing with
them, how to be forgiving to the thoughtless and gentle with the erring,
how to be large-minded amid small-mindedness, how to endure discourtesy
and grow in courtesy oneself, and so on.

It will be seen that I am not talking at all of packaged information as ridiculed by critics of the banking concept of education. There
is a sort of packaging, but the packages are people. To meet Tom
Sawyer, Anne of Green Gables, to live with them through the slow and
extended experience of a book (the slowness is rather important), to
have identified with them, to have grown in the effort, all this is
worlds apart from mere packaged information and even from formulated
judgments of value.

The examples given already suggest the means of communicating
these values and judgments, that substitute temporarily in the pupil for
personal wisdom, personal knowledge, personal understanding, personal
experience: the means is literature. Here the young come to know those
notable people of fiction who are as real for present purposes as one's
next-door neighbor, and more broadening for one's education. They stock

their minds and hearts with figures that will function as ideal types, as their own experience widens and the possibility of understanding emerges. In this sense they come, through literature, to know their own resources, their own limitations, the makeup of their consciousness, the passions that erupt, the means of control, the stern decisions, options, crossroads to be encountered—simply because they have received as a gift from tradition a world of people who embody this "knowledge" and not at all because the knowledge is immanently generated.

There comes to mind here a remark which I believe I heard in Lonergan's lectures on education, though I cannot verify that, to the effect that the real arbiters of morality are the artists, in the sense that it is they who form the mores of a people and the race. Let me repeat a quotation I have already used from Insight: art "in its subtler forms ... is content to communicate any of the moods in which ... questions [on humanity] arise, to convey any of the tones in which they may be answered or ignored."[11] This I find illuminating on what an artist is about. But now we have to add that artists, like everyone else, live and work in an existential situation in which they cannot evade responsibility for the creation of a people's values and judgments. As Lonergan said recently in response to a question about violence in movies, there is violence in Sophocles too, but violence that raises profound moral questions, not violence that merely provides two hours of diversion for an empty mind.[12] The point is not to have an antiseptic literature; Newman has shown what an illusion that is: "It is a contradiction in terms to attempt a sinless Literature of sinful man."[13] Nor is the point to have the "good guys" and the "bad guys" carefully labeled for our easy and simplistic identification with the former. The point is that a literature in which ideals do not appear at all, in which the trend is massively toward portraying characters who are simply a-moral, is exploring the human with a myopic eye. By all means let Marion Engel be free to explore the possibilities of a love affair with

---

11. Lonergan, Insight, p. 185.

12. This was at the Boston College Lonergan Workshop, June, 1982; I quote from memory.

13. John Henry Newman, The Idea of a University Defined and Illustrated (London: Longmans, Green and Co., 1929), p. 229.

a bear, and Marie Blais to recount her dreary experiences in the under-
world. But is there no Dickens to give us a Sydney Carton, no Hawthorne
to give us the minister, sinning but courageously repentant, of The
Scarlet Letter? We need them too, and desperately.

It is time to talk of understanding, and its role in development
from above downward. My position has been that values can be handed
over and received in love and trust, that, even though not personally
generated, they can become effective in the control of one's life. I
have taken the same position on judgments: that they can be formed on
the basis of values received, as well as accepted in a more blanket
fashion on the basis of belief in another; and that, when received in
this way, even though not personally generated, they can be operative in
life, serve as guides, provide us with a view of ourselves and our
world.

But the same cannot be said of understanding. It cannot be given
by one person to another (special divine gifts excepted). Understanding
has to be personally achieved. That does not mean it plays no role in
the development that begins from above, but the role is somewhat complex. More so than appeared in chapter two when we talked of the
Socratic role of the teacher in helping the pupil form the fertile image
to produce the insight. We can see that process more clearly now in its
complexity: the act of understanding occurs in the upward movement of
the pupil, but it is assisted from above, by an understanding already
formed (in another, however) and moving in the downward path of
tradition.

Further, we have come to a very special case of such assistance
from above to a development from below, namely, the teacher's role in
helping the pupil to understand the need and process of tradition
itself. Tradition as a category, just as much as a theorem in geometry,
is a "whatness" to be understood; there are data for the one problem as
there are for the other; and the teacher's role, in the one case as in
the other, is to help the pupil arrange the data, form the fertile
image, and so achieve insight. Let us not be afraid of simplicity here,
and so I propose a little model lesson on tradition on the occasion of
teaching the poem mentioned earlier, "Who Has Seen the Wind?" The poem
is a treasured part of our patrimony, preserved and handed on in tradition; the objective is to help the pupil see that as a value. The
teacher might ask, Have you any treasures from the past at home? How

old is the oldest? How did it come to be kept? And how old is this
poem? How did it come to us today? Can you picture the empty place in
our literature if earlier generations had not kept it and handed it on?
And so on.

The poem is an example of the beautiful received as part of the
pupil's heritage. But myriad humdrum truths are received in the same
way, as part of a system of beliefs on which we depend daily and hourly
without adverting to them. It will be the educator's business to see
that the pupil does advert to them; as we draw a triangle to aid understanding of a geometry problem, so we will adduce the pupils' experience
to show them how much they depend on belief, to show how the world's
business would grind to a halt without a continual and pervasive use of
trust in another's word and acceptance of what we do not know on our
own. Such teaching is the more needed in the measure that it is so
regularly neglected. As Lonergan says about our schools:

> Students are encouraged to find things out for themselves, to
> develop originality, to be creative, to criticize, but it does
> not seem that they are instructed in the enormous role of belief
> in the acquisition and the expansion of knowledge. Many do not
> seem to be aware that what they know of science is not immanent-
> ly generated but for the most part simply belief.[14]

One could usefully start with the multiple trust shown in the world
about one, before one is up an hour in the morning: that the community
will follow normal time-schedules; that buses will run their normal
routes; that when my mother says, It is raining, her words mean what I
have taken them to mean in the past. The possibilities are endless, and
only preliminary to the more academic beliefs, a host of which are in
operation before I have been in the classroom an hour: that water is
composed of oxygen and hydrogen; that the nation's war leader was such
and such a person; that the high tides today are due to the sun and moon
pulling in the same direction; and so forth. Now all of these may be in
one way or another "verifiable," some with ease, some with difficulty,
some only in an analogous sense. But that is not the point; the point
is that the pupil accepts them, does so without question, regards it as
quite reasonable to accept them. And then perhaps maintains as a

---

14. Lonergan, "The Response of the Jesuit as Priest and Apostle in the
    Modern World," A Second Collection, pp. 185-86.

principle, having been taught to do so by radical educators (that is, having accepted their word for it), that the function of school is to let pupils "find things out for themselves, to develop originality, to be creative, to criticize."

Let us check our bearings. I have been arguing that both tradition and belief are values embodied in experience, and that teachers can assist the pupil to understand this experience, just as they can assist in the understanding of geometry. Now there is a further point: I can apply my wonder not only to the experienced data but also to an accepted truth. I can wonder not only about the spectrum of colors in the oil slick I see, or about the data on tradition and belief as institutions; I can also wonder about the content of particular truths received from tradition and on trust. "He that loses his life shall find it." Suppose I believe this on the word of One I trust, and believe that it is applicable to my own conduct, indeed important for my own making of myself. But how can I apply it to my conduct if I do not understand it? Once again I can understand only by assembling data and letting my wonder play upon them, but once again too it is a dynamism operating from above that evokes my wonder.

The example I gave will be recognized as a religious truth, but the principle holds over a far wider field than the religious. It means nothing less than Newman's readiness to believe, maintained as an antecedent attitude, as opposed to skepticism as an antecedent attitude.[15] Let me quote here a remark known well enough by ascetical masters but known less well in academe. It may indeed be met only with scorn by those who train debaters to go for the jugular in debate, and by their counterparts in the world of philosophy; but, if so, that would only indicate to me how sadly neglected the way of heritage is in much education. The remark was prefaced to his Spiritual Exercises by St. Ignatius Loyola, and runs as follows.

> The presupposition here is that any good Christian ought to be more ready to save his neighbor's proposition than to condemn it; and, if he cannot save it, let him inquire how it is to be understood.[16]

---

15. Newman, Grammar of Assent, p. 377.

16. I have translated the Latin of the Thesaurus Spiritualis Societatis Jesu (Bruges: Desclée de Brouwer, 1932), pp. 32-33. In the numbering of the later, definitive edition (see the appendix below), the 'presupposition' is paragraph 22.

The significance of this for daily life is pervasive. Possibly we know all too well the type of person characterized by negativity, a disposition to dispute everything, to put difficulties in the way of every proposal, to find fault with suggestions of others while contributing no positive alternative, the type in short with whom to live and work is simply a cross. And so the question occurs: if we find negativity so unproductive in daily life, should we not at least inquire whether it may be similarly barren in the schools? It may be, or it may not be, but have we ever asked the question whether it is? Some concrete examples: do we read a book primarily to see where we can find the author wrong, or primarily to see what the author may teach us? And, when we come upon an argument or position that is unexpected or puzzling, do we look for the weakness, error perhaps? Or do we look for a point that had lain outside our horizon, one we now have the opportunity to learn? If we accept the general principle of a development from above, we may find food for thought in the remark of Ignatius. We may also note the difference between the belligerent attitude and the learner's, and the sense in which Lonergan says that understanding develops by encountering, not the familiar, but the puzzling.[17]

Understanding, to return to our basic point, must wait on experience of life, if it is to be real and not merely notional; for it is understanding of data on reality as opposed to data on words, and data on reality accumulate slowly in experience of life, a day at a time, over long years. There is no possibility of compressing it into the sort of instant process that is much favored today for making coffee, taking a photograph, and the like; there is no instant experience (the reader may recall my earlier remark about the long novel, and its importance for our slowly developing acquaintance with its characters).[18]

---

17. Lonergan, De intellectu et methodo, pp. 21-22 (of a 72-page, legal-size set of mimeographed notes by students reporting on a course offered by Lonergan in the spring semester, 1959, to doctoral students at the Gregorian University in Rome).

18. The old-style reading at meals in religious communities was extraordinarily effective, not just because it was heard in common and regularly discussed later, but also because it was received slowly day by day—there was time to grow in refinement of appreciation.

Without such experience the pupil may indeed acquire what
Lonergan calls, after St. Thomas Aquinas, a scientia nominis that will
enable him or her to talk, even to debate quite creditably, but not to
hold in his or her grasp a scientia rei or real apprehension of himself
or herself and his or her world.   The dangers of this period and state
of life have been set forth by Newman in speaking of the awful superficiality (what he calls "viewiness") which especially afflicts the
young.

> [A]t first they have no principles laid down within them as a
> foundation for the intellect to build upon; they have no dis-
> criminating convictions, and no grasp of consequences. And
> therefore they talk at random, if they talk much, and cannot
> help being flippant, or what is emphatically called 'young.'
> They are merely dazzled by phenomena, instead of perceiving
> things as they are.

With this he contrasts the case "When the intellect has once been
properly trained and formed to have a connected view or grasp of
things." The effect can then be seen "in the good sense, sobriety of
thought, reasonableness, candour, self-command, and steadiness of view,
which characterize it." He is concerned to show that when he speaks "so
much of the formation, and consequent grasp, of the intellect" he is not
advocating "that spurious philosophism, which shows itself in what, for
want of a word, I may call 'viewiness' ... brilliant general views about
all things whatever."[19]

Newman's point is the lack of training and discipline of the
youthful mind, where mine is its lack of experience. Still, the cases
are close enough for us to derive support and wisdom from his position.
Some of us may recall our own youth and the awful superficiality of the
great general views we were wont to hold and pompously set forth (in our
daydreams anyway) before a breathless world.   I have such memories myself, and I cringe to recall them: "views" on communism, on the church,
on political parties, on nations and their characteristics, on youth and
age, on the conventions of society, and so on.

One more example, in a much more serious matter. Kierkegaard, in
the Concluding Unscientific Postscript, provides topics on which we
might attempt, each of us, to take an existential attitude. One of them

---

19. Newman, Idea of a University, pp. xvi, xvii, xviii.

is death: what does it mean that I (I myself, not the human race in
general) am on the way to death? I have tried with a theology class to
achieve and express such an existential attitude, and with Kierkegaard
we found it almost impossible. But let a day of sickness overtake us,
when life seems fragile, when dire thoughts of troubles within spring to
mind, when the future is suddenly uncertain, and what a difference it
makes in our "apprehension" of this age-old truth, that we are going to
die.

Our discussion of the role of understanding in the development
which follows the way of heritage has involved us naturally and almost
insensibly in discussion of the level of experience. So it remains only
to round off this fourth subheading, and ask what the educator can do to
assist in the business of adding experience to experience in a cumula-
tive growth that will eventually change notional apprehension into real.
Much experience, of course, merely happens and is not subject to control
from above. So it ought to be, and nevertheless educator and parent can
contribute needed guidance in the accumulation of both direct and vicarious experience. The latter is simpler: it is a matter of providing
books, music and art, television programs and movies, plays and novels,
and so on. I have little to add to the wisdom of parents and educators
here; they will know, better than I do, what gems are available and what
junk, and with what fatal ease the choice of junk can become a habit.
But perhaps I may say a word in defense of the "classics" of literature.
They have a bad name in some circles, where putting them on the reading
program is seen as forcing dulness on the young when interesting books
and stories are at hand instead.   I think the matter may not be so
simple. Besides immediate "interest" there are long-range "interests"
and the pupil can hardly be expected to appreciate the latter. I will
speak in chapter five of my regular advice to writers of doctoral dis-
sertations, that often "to meet interesting questions, one has to begin
from quite uninteresting ones."[20]   Is something analogous to be said
about a school reading program? Not dulness for the sake of dulness as
a criterion of choice; but not simply immediate interest either, which
might be captured by the titillation of four-letter words and the
exciting feeling of the pupils that they are reading what their parents

---

20. Lonergan, Insight, pp. 173-174.

are reading. The true criterion is surely neither dulness nor titillation, but the treasury of human possibilities opened up to the pupil by
the magic key of books, and some of these possibilities are to be discovered only with a little labor.

Books offer vicarious experience, but there is also the direct
experience one may gain through travel, a hunting expedition with one's
father, a family get-together, games and parties, and the like. Obvious
here, I suppose, is the special need to be sensitive to the needs and
excitement of the young, for what to parent may be a bore can be of the
highest interest to them. Less obvious may be the value of relating
personal experience to vicarious. I remember still the moment in one of
our boyhood expeditions when our father, on reaching a high point in the
semi-mountainous terrain, turned and searched the southwest horizon.
"Look," he said, "you can see Cassidy Lake from here." I looked and
saw, and could have gazed for hours. It was not just the normal thrill
of exploration, of seeing across the miles a lake of which I had heard
so often; it was the thrill, deeper than I can now express in words, of
poetry learned at school suddenly coming vividly alive, of Sir Walter
Scott's experience of long ago and far away, leaping across the centuries and the oceans to become mine:

> I climb'd the dark brow of the mighty Helvellyn;
>   Lakes and mountains beneath me gleam'd misty and wide;
> All was still, save by fits, when the eagle was yelling,
>   And starting around me the echoes replied.

I heard no eagle, nor was one needed. The moment remains, a rare combination of personal and vicarious experience, as one of the treasures
in my data bank, my personal history museum, a moment I can relive over
and over when it comes back to

> flash upon that inward eye
> Which is the bliss of solitude.

This occurrence simply happened; it was fortuitous. But could
not much more be done somewhat systematically? I suppose there is a
sort of semi-systematic effort along these lines, as when the teacher
prepares the class to visit a museum or a historic site, or when a

family reads travelogues and history before setting out on its travels
during vacation. May the ideas I have tried to express here assist them
to bring such efforts into perspective and focus. I have to be content,
as so often in this book, with presenting a heuristic notion that may
stimulate thinking for those who are in the field and in a position to
conceive the practical insights.

CHAPTER FOUR

THE INTEGRATED WAY:

"EX PARTITA VITA IN UNITAM CONSURGERE"

The ideal human development is not a growth from experience
through understanding and judgment to responsibly chosen values and
decisive action. Neither is it a matter of receiving values in a way of
life handed down in a community, and holding views accepted in faith
till maturity gives understanding and experience becomes informed by
that understanding. The ideal human development is the integration of
the two, and their use in interrelation with one another:

> These two modes of development are interdependent. Both
> begin from infancy. But only through the second does the first
> take one beyond the earliest prehistoric stages of human
> development. Only through the first is there any real assimila-
> tion and appropriation of the second.
> Such interdependence, as it supposes distinction, so too it
> opposes separation ...[1]

Hence, what I have put asunder in chapters two and three I must now join
back together. Only we must remember that we are not dealing with a
simple conceptual distinction, with two ideas first set forth in
separate chapters and then reunited in another. Behind that mental
exercise lies a conflict of real forces with a real breakdown of unity
in human living. It is, therefore, a real unity that we seek. To that
end it will be helpful to examine first the breakdown, then proceed in
two steps to integration: the unity we envision, and the means whereby
that unity may be achieved.

---

1. Bernard Lonergan, "Questionnaire on Philosophy," Method: Journal of
   Lonergan Studies 2 (1984), no. 2, p. 10. This set of responses was
   written in 1976 on request, to aid a symposium of Jesuit philosophers
   at Villa Cavalletti (near Rome), held September 8-18, 1977.

89

1. Collapse of Peaceful Coexistence

An old bit of Scholastic philosophy made unity one of the
transcendental concepts: as each thing is good and true, so is it also
one. God alone, however, is the highest good, the fulness of truth, the
undivided unity; the creature, as it is imperfectly good and true, is
also imperfectly one. Further, the created form of unity has a fluctu-
ating history: it can disintegrate, but it can also grow stronger.
Thus, Thomas Aquinas made the perfection of the spiritual life consist
in the rise from a divided to a unified state of life: "ex partita vita
in unitam consurgere."[2] In the same way I will maintain that one of
the main problems in education is to overcome the conflict that inevita-
bly arises between the two vector forces we found operative there. In
fact, it can be argued quite plausibly that only out of such conflict
encountered head-on and overcome will true unity be forged. For we are
not really dealing with an original innocent unity that later falls
apart. The child, it is true, gives the appearance of a unified and
undivided consciousness, but only the appearance. The unity is unexamined, untested, ungrounded; there is no sense of two forces at work
which will one day conflict. Adolescents make that discovery, but have
not yet the will, wisdom, and means to integrate them. So the educator
has the task of helping them to understand their situation and to work
toward a unity that is not just the restoration of a peaceful coexistence but a new creation in young people fully alive to the diverse
factors at work in them, from themselves and from their environment.

We begin by accepting the commonplace that adolescence is the
period of most apparent conflict. But let us accept that in a neutral
attitude, not naming it tendentiously (for example, the period of contempt for authority) or apportioning praise and blame, but thinking of
it under the general headings that have structured this work so far.

------

2. Here Thomas refers to Dionysius, the Areopagite (as he was thought to
   be): "Dionysius perfectum sanctitatis semper designat per hoc quod
   est ex partita vita in unitam consurgere" (In I Sententiarum, d. 17,
   q. 2, a. 2, sol.).

A first step is to recognize the biological factors that work in some independence from the educational.   The onset of puberty is manifestly a potent factor in young people's discovery of their self-identity and their need for self-assertion.   Moreover, since this is a universal phenomenon, it can reasonably be invoked as a chief factor in the conflict between heritage and achievement;   since it is likewise a phenomenon occurring, with some variations, at about the same age in all peoples, it can be invoked too as the factor that locates the breakdown in so many cases during entry into teenage.

The matter is not, however, quite so simple. Biological factors may be more or less the same everywhere, but social, cultural and educational influences vary enormously; in one people they may achieve at six what in another people does not occur at sixty. Is there any reason for them to have their maximum effect at teenage? Why should there be coincidence, as there seems to be, despite the immense difference in cultures, between attitudes developing out of education and attitudes developing out of new biological and physiological influences? Of course, there are extremely stable societies in which our Western pattern of conflict and rebellion does not really occur in noticeable form. The young may be admitted through initiating rites into adulthood, but they do not really take control over their lives; this is exercised rather by age-old tradition, interpreted naturally enough by those who have lived it longest.   But in our Western society conflict occurs, and with all our progress it continues to occur around the same age. Why?

On a first level the answer is obvious enough: it is our educational system that makes rebellion occur, but it is the biological factor that makes it occur at puberty.   Items of knowledge which, considered abstractly, are the same at age six as at age sixteen, are not the same at all when considered in the concrete learner subject to biological growth. But we can give this a deeper basis through Newman's distinction between notional and real apprehension of one and the same truth. Notional propositions, he argued, use common nouns, standing for what is abstract ("Man is mortal"), and our apprehension of these is also notional. But in "real" propositions the terms stand for what is unit and individual ("Philip was the father of Alexander"), and our apprehension of them is real.   Now the same proposition, he continues,

may have a notional sense for a schoolboy and a real sense for a better
informed person:

> "Dulce et decorum est pro patria mori," is a mere commonplace ...
> if Philippi is to be the index of ... patriotism, whereas it
> would be the record of experiences, a sovereign dogma, a grand
> aspiration, inflaming the imagination, piercing the heart, of a
> Wallace or a Tell.[3]

The difference Newman saw between a poet, writing at a distance on the
glory of dying for one's country, and the patriot, ready to sacrifice
actual life, is the difference we all experience, under other headings,
between childhood and adolescence.   The efficacy of education, in other
words, is severely limited in the young by biology.

     We should try to be precise on this point. There are geniuses,
it seems, who are composing symphonies or doing university mathematics
at the age of seven, and I do not dispute that educators will be able to
lower the age at which such activities occur, if not to produce
geniuses. But the kind of experience involved in the data base for
mathematics is extremely narrow in comparison with the development now
in question. For I am speaking of experience of oneself and one's
neighbors, experience of world, of life, of time; I am speaking both of
direct experience of living with others, working and quarreling and
being reconciled with them, and also of the vicarious experience the
young begin to have, and a scholar or connoisseur may gain through long
and thorough acquaintance, with art, history, literature. And I am
thinking of all this experience interpreted by a consciousness that
suffers a quantum leap in interior development when, at entry into the
teens, the young discover new possibilities, a whole new world for
exploration.

     Meanwhile, the intervening years will have taught them to use
words, to put ideas in order, to stand on their feet and have their say,
to take part in the democratic processes of the classroom. They will be
getting ready, under educational and cultural influences, to think for
themselves, to judge for themselves, to decide for themselves. They
await only that emergence of the self which puberty so effectively
determines, for that readiness to turn to action. Now the pupil, conscious of power to achieve, begins to feel as a burden the system of

---

3. Newman, Grammar of Assent, pp. 9-10.

values and views received as heritage, and starts a rebellion that will
be more or less violent against the establishment.

Newman spoke of real and notional "apprehension," declining to
use the word "understanding."[4] In our analysis of the situation understanding is the key concept, in the sense defined in chapter one, for it
is the meeting-point of development from below with development from
above. As I maintained earlier, values and judgments may be given and
received, but understanding may not. Understanding can be guided in one
person by the dynamism of someone else's knowledge operating from above,
but understanding as occurring is always a personal achievement, related
to its base in that person's experience. Now experience accumulates,
first in a slow process, then rapidly with the leap into puberty; at
this time what was merely notional understanding in a key area becomes
real understanding, and youth turns a critical eye on former views and
values.

We may image the resulting conflict, thinking, for example, of
two trains heading toward one another on the same track, or of our
satellite shooting off into space when the balance of the vector forces
is lost. Images are to be used insofar as they help. More prosaic, but
more explanatory, is the notion of dependence: the way of heritage
bespeaks a large measure of dependence in the pupil, the way of achievement means the gaining of independence. But the key element of explanation is the linking of accumulating experience and growing understanding
to a set of values and judgments received earlier in trust and now
coming under scrutiny. From this viewpoint the possibility of conflict
is built-in, whether one sees it from the standpoint of authority and
calls it rebellion, or from that of developing youth and calls it self-
realization.

What is built-in and therefore natural still admits infinite
variety. Here one might open a profitable discussion of the diverse
"social characters" and their incidence and history in different
peoples.[5] In a more modest approach one could inquire into the variety

---

4. Newman, Grammar of Assent, pp. 19-20.

5. It was impossible for me to incorporate the wealth of insights on
   education in David Riesman (with Nathan Glazer and Reuel Denney), The
   Lonely Crowd: A Study of the Changing American Character (New Haven:
   Yale University Press, 1950; abridged pb ed., New York: Doubleday,
   1953).

of ways the young manifest their independence in everyday life. I would
think, for example, that it would show up first in the home, with regard
to domestic discipline: attendance at meals, hours of retiring and
rising, and so on; but those who defy a parent may still listen quite
subserviently to a favorite professor; and so on. My concern is still
with the built-in constants, rather than the variables; if it is true
that built-in factors supply the potential for conflict, it is also true
that they can be guided to fuller cooperation. That will occupy us in
our next sections.

2. Integration: The Goal

Our theme is integration, moving from an unexamined coexistence
through analyzed breakdown to a grounded unity. To this end it will
help to look ahead to the sort of product we hope for from education, an
ideal type of the mature person. Some readers will protest vehemently
against such a procedure as a suppression of the pupil's personal
creativity. But their opposition to us need not be diametric. Realization of personal creativity, after all, is itself a goal of sorts. If
some educators prefer not to define the goal too precisely, surely they
would not exclude from it our basic precepts: Be attentive, be intelligent, be reasonable, be responsible, be loving toward others. Those
precepts define our mature person, who will be something like the
"genuine" person of Insight[6] and the "authentic" person of Method.[7]

In this ideal type the understanding, views, and values the
student has acquired in the upward movement from experience will be in
substantial accord with those developed in the downward movement from
tradition. The accord will not mean an unconditional surrender of
either side to the other, of tradition to achievement, or of achievement
to tradition. But the tradition will have been purified, with mythic
elements better understood, legendary untruths corrected, biases overcome, narrow horizons broadened; this side of the picture is not to be
glossed over with pious creeds affirming unchanging human nature, or

---

6. Lonergan, Insight, pp. 475–478.

7. Lonergan, Method; see the Index under "authenticity."

with reverent and unexamined acceptance of what our ancestors did. And, on the other side, half-formed ideals, shallow judgments, insubstantial values, all the phenomena that are apt to show in the slow appropriation of one's universe, will have been moderated by the conservative force of tradition, and themselves subjected to the self-correcting process which is the essence of learning; by the same token judgments and values retained from tradition will have been given a personal basis and a foundation that tradition itself cannot supply.

In other words, one-time pupils will have grown to the point where they are themselves and not copies of someone else, where they are persons of principle, at peace with the true values of both tradition and the contemporary world. At peace with the values of tradition, toward which, in a spirit of reform but not of radical disloyalty, they will have modified their affective state, coming to realize better the integrity of intention in parent, nation, church, and to take a more compassionate attitude when they find that integrity flawed. At peace also with the values of the contemporary world, not living with faces turned to the past but as people of their times, moved by and moving with and contributing to the spirit of the times, open and yet critical, accepting what is good, challenging what is pernicious.

A parallel situation will obtain on the level of judgment. The person of mature equilibrium will have revised many a judgment that family, clan, nation, church, has handed on; again, revised it not in disloyalty but in the recognition of the imperfection of all knowledge, in acceptance of Newman's dictum that to live is to change and to be perfect is to have changed often.[8] But the process will not have been simply one of critical destruction. Adolescents coming to maturity will also have come to see what they could not possibly have seen earlier, that there is wisdom in views they were too ready to discard; they will have come to a real apprehension of much that was accepted in faith, with only a notional apprehension at best, in childhood. So their minds, like their hearts, will be at peace with the universe. Which is a way of saying that one's own universe is more or less in coincidence with the universe. Near enough to coincidence, at any rate, to elimi-nate fear of total disruption. Finally, the whole development comes

---

8. John Henry Newman, An Essay on the Development of Christian Doctrine (New York: Doubleday pb., 1960) p. 63.

more and more under the sign of love, as one grows toward peace with
one's fellows, first in the community of educators and pupils, expanding
the community of home and clan, then in the community of the human race,
when the simple delight of the child in what is, has been transformed
into adult content to be in Mitsein with all humankind. If this kind of
love is not always listed among the goals of education, is that a point
against my position, or against those listings?   Love, then, as it was
the original gift in the way of heritage, is also the crowning element
in the way of achievement.

        Neither original gift, however, nor crowning achievement is the
key transitional factor in the development from child, through pupil and
student, to mature citizen. The key factor here is understanding, made
possible now from adolescence onward by a sufficient accumulation of
experience, and a sufficiently trained intellect to deal discriminating-
ly and methodically with the data. This sufficiency, be it noted, is an
analogous term.   Philosophers will not achieve personal integration,
coincidence between their universe and the universe, equilibrium between
what they receive and what they create, unless they have had long
exposure to, and grappled with, the great thinkers.   But simple old
souls who have never heard of Plato or Aristotle may achieve peace with
the universe in a simple way corresponding to the simplicity of their
development and character. That is, they may recognize that their universe is narrow, but achieve coincidence with the universe by the simple
expedient of relying on pastor, doctor, lawyer, all of whom they trust,
to take care of matters that may concern them but are beyond their ken.
But I suppose that in this business of education, we are not usually
dealing with this sort of genuinely authentic but very unsophisticated
person.

        I have been talking of the individually genuine and authentic
person we might envisage, without prejudice to personal creativity and
self-expression, as the goal of education.   But we live in communities
that divide into the leaders and the led, more sharply in totalitarian
countries, less sharply in democracies.   Leadership thus becomes an
analogous term, tending to tyranny at one extreme and to merely representative functions at the other.   But in between there is room for
leadership, understood broadly as influence, so I may be asked how my
strategy of education relates to that fact. The request will not be for
a review of the whole question but only for its relation to our topic.

The first element in my answer is almost predetermined: there will be two types of leader, depending on whether the dominant factor in the situation is achievement or heritage. In the former the creative and expansive moment is the emergence of the idea, and the leadership will be operative for good or for ill depending basically on the depth of the idea, its reference to reality, its promise for what is truly worth while. But when the heritage is dominant, the basic factor will be the character of the leader, and the degree in which the leader stands as symbol for the values and beliefs of the community.

This first and basic element admits in both cases of many variations. The creative idea may be worked out in years of isolated study in the Library of the British Museum, to take effect a century later in the attraction of half the world to Marxism. Or it may become immediately operative on the public scene, as in the Marshall Plan for the reconstruction of post-war Europe. As for the role of the traditional leader, this will not be the same in a time of national crisis as it is in a humdrum period of history. Again, the potential leader may be gifted, this too in either of our two basic categories, with extraordinary personal qualities, a power of persuasion, a charisma, that give more than usual efficacy to the leadership. Or there may be leaders of the quiet type, who slowly build up a following in virtue of steady performance. My concern here, as always, is not with the variables; it is to include this important aspect in the general goal of education, and to relate it to our two basic ways of development.

There is a further aspect that regards more the character of a people than the qualities of a leader, and this too can be related to our two ways of development. Take the two types that might be symbolized by American efficiency and British muddling through. The first seems to fall more readily under the heading of upward development, as specified and characterized by an emphasis on planning: one collects the data, orders the questions, guides decision-making through principles of group dynamics, and so on. The other seems to fall under the heading of downward development; it is characterized by holding fast to the tradition while keeping a stiff upper lip in time of chaos. On paper the advantage seems to be altogether on the side of American efficiency, to the point that one might even question whether British muddling through is a way of development at all. All the same, planning can become an obsession: there is planning, planning, and more planning, till

creativity is stifled.   There   may   well   be   room at times for muddled
planning and creative chaos.   At any rate, whether one plans well,
muddles firmly, or attempts a happy combination of the two, the two ways
of human development may furnish guidelines for eventual integration.

This whole section has been concerned with "ideal types" that may
not exist in reality. It could be argued that they are not only ideal
but idyllic, not only unreal but impossible, set forth in terms so naive
as to forfeit any claim to attention. Let us agree that the equilibrium
I posit as goal is only relative. Lonergan keeps insisting how precar-
ious the achievement of authenticity is,[9] and his caution is especially
pertinent here. Bereavements, tragedies, personal crises, keep occurring in the human community: there is family breakup, financial
disaster, religious doubt and waywardness and, more insidious than any
of these, the creeping inauthenticity of the daily round. Experience,
understanding, reflection, decision and the formation of values, all are
to go forward daily then, but in continual and ongoing struggle. The
"system" of dynamic consciousness is not a static system. There is a
wheel that keeps turning, not as a flywheel does, remaining put, but as
the wheel of a chariot does, and maybe a "chariot of fire":

> I will not cease from mental fight
>   Nor shall my sword sleep in my hand,
> Till we have built Jerusalem
>   In England's green and pleasant land.

—But perhaps chapter five would be a better locus for discussion of
such ongoing adult formation.

3. Integration: The Means

If the goal of education, described in these general terms, is a
legitimate ideal, if the "product" of education, conceived in this heuristic way, is a person in whom the creative impulse has not been stifled
but rather strengthened, it is in place to speak of the means by which
the integration of the vector forces bearing on development may be
achieved.

---

9. For example, see Lonergan, Method, pp. 110, 252, 284.

But, since our focal concern is the crisis situation of adolescence, we should distinguish here between ordinary slow, gradual growth
and the sudden, sharper changes which may be so radical as to constitute
a revolution in one's living. Let me speak for a moment of my father's
way of growing tomatoes and cabbage, as I remember it years later. In
early spring he planted the seeds in small boxes of earth set in the
sunny window of the kitchen. The seedlings came up in thick profusion,
crowding one another in their cramped quarters. So in the next stage he
took the stronger plants, set them farther apart in larger boxes and,
the weather being now a bit warmer, put them outdoors, though still
under glass, in a sheltered area. The last stage, when the plants had
grown so much as to crowd one another again, was to set them out in the
garden with ample room to reach their final growth.—It is a simple
instance of the difference between gradual growth and radical change in
the conditions of growth. More mechanically minded readers may prefer
to think of shifting gears: one picks up speed, but only to a limited
extent, in low gear; then one shifts to a higher, only to encounter a
similar limit; and so on, in a process that may be repeated endlessly in
mechanics.

I use these examples to illustrate the different modes of growth
that occur in the educational process too. At the same time they raise
the question in a new way of the role of the educator: that role will
assume greater importance, obviously, at the point of radical transition
than in gradual day-to-day growth. But, before coming to that role, let
us get a firmer grasp on the kind of transition occurring at adolescence. The change involved is very much like that which Lonergan
describes under the heading of conversion:

> By conversion is understood a transformation of the subject
> and his world. Normally it is a prolonged process though its
> explicit acknowledgment may be concentrated in a few momentous
> judgments and decisions. Still it is not just a development or
> even a series of developments. Rather it is a resultant change
> of course and direction. It is as if one's eyes were opened and
> one's former world faded and fell away. There emerges something
> new that fructifies in inter-locking, cumulative sequences of
> developments on all levels and in all departments of human
> living.[10]

---

10. Lonergan, Method, p. 130.

It is true that Lonergan distinguishes conversion in this sense from genetic development,[11] and adolescence would seem to fall more naturally into the latter class. Still, the changes involved are so radical as to share many of the characteristics of conversion. This becomes clear when we reflect what a major step adolescence is in the process of becoming oneself. Let me quote Lonergan on that process as well:

> The subject has more and more to do with his own becoming ...
> Development is a matter of increasing the number of things that
> one does for oneself, that one decides for oneself, that one
> finds out for oneself. Parents and teachers and professors and
> superiors let people do more and more for themselves, decide
> more and more for themselves, find out more and more for them-
> selves.
>   There is a critical point in the increasing autonomy of the
> subject. It is reached when the subject finds out for himself
> that it is up to himself to decide what he is to make of him-
> self.[12]

This great step Lonergan labels the "existential discovery":

> [T]he development of knowledge and the development of moral
> feeling head to the existential discovery, the discovery of
> oneself as a moral being, the realization that one not only
> chooses between courses of action but also thereby makes oneself
> an authentic human being or an unauthentic one.[13]

Adolescents, I would say, are going through the radical transition that will enable them, perhaps years later and after long reflection, to reach the critical point of existential discovery.

It is here, I have said, that the role of the teacher assumes new importance and is exercised in a different mode. Where that role, in the periods of gradual growth, may be exercised as a spur or a gentle

---

11. See Lonergan, Method, p. 236, on genetic and dialectical differ-
    ences; on dialectical differences as requiring conversion, see pp.
    224, 237-244, 251-253, 287.

12. Lonergan, "Existenz and Aggiornamento," Collection: Papers by
    Bernard Lonergan, S.J., edited by F. E. Crowe (New York: Herder and
    Herder, 1967), pp. 240-251; quotation at pp. 241-242.

13. Lonergan, Method, p. 38. Note his remark in Collection, p. 242: "In
    this life the critical point is never transcended." See also note
    9, above.

rein, it becomes in transition to adulthood a much more delicate matter. It is just here, likewise, that the role of systems and machines proves negligible; it is the personal influence of the teacher that is needed. The situation, in fact, becomes paradoxical: pupils are to be freed from their heritage, in the sense of being given control of their own future, but at the same time they are to receive this control, in some degree, as part of their heritage, so one might say that their last hereditary right is to be set free from their heritage.

It is time to turn from general remarks to concrete details, structured again according to our analysis of consciousness. On the level, then, of experience, adolescents are going to read the books, see the movies, associate with the friends, enjoy the holiday, and so on, that they themselves choose. On the level of understanding, they are going to turn from the study of words to the study of things;[14] they will want to know, not just what words mean in books, but how things work in reality: radio, motorcar, whatever. On the level of reflection, they will develop views—very critical they are apt to be too—on parents, teachers, church, community. On the fourth level they will be making their own decisions on daily occupations and, more fundamentally, will be thinking of what to do with life: the whole dazzling world, through "magic casements," is opening before them; the possibilities are diverse and numberless, and they must choose.

There will then be a process of critiquing values and judgments previously accepted, either to abandon them or to give them a foundation in the adolescent's consciousness that they had lacked before. So how will the teacher enter into this process? I suppose somewhat as follows. A poem that was once taught in order to release the pupil's fantasy, or to store mind and heart with beauty, might now be examined for the poet's position on social or political questions; I remember well the jolt it was to my consciousness forty years ago when the beauty of Virgil's Aeneid had captured my imagination, and I then attended a lecture on "Virgil's Minority Report," to discover the world of politics in which he wrote. Again the history that inducted the pupil into a

---

14. Words, of course, are in their own way also "things," and can quite properly become the object of study at the highest level. I am not, therefore, saying that a professor of semiotics is merely doing what young pupils do in lower grades.

community extending over generations, that fostered pride in one's
nation and its great men and women, might now become material for new
questions: on the nation's guilt, on the incompetence of its military
leaders, on the human weakness of the founding fathers. Similarly,
accepted cultural values might now be questioned—the Swiss work ethic
challenged by an Irish ethic of leisure!

Such general lines of transition are easy enough to determine,
once we accept the two ways of development, and the sequence internal to
each. More difficult, however, is the time schedule for the transitions. In chapter five I will say something on the specific transition
proper to the university, but really the main thing for me is the direction and quality of the change, and not such secondary questions as
whether a step belongs in high school or university. In any case, I
would expect considerable leeway here, so that the educator might have
to think of a flexible schedule of operations for helping the pupil move
from reliance on others to reliance on self. Thus parents, I hope,
allow their children to "believe" in Santa Claus, stocking the childish
imagination with delightful fantasies and promoting a sense of ultimate
goodness in the universe; but I would not try to determine for them the
point at which the reality principle should displace, as gently as may
be, the fantasy world. Again, I am sure a child could listen in sheer
wonder and delight to Tolkien's stories of the hobbits, and equally sure
that an adult can hardly read The Lord of the Rings without great questions of good and evil, passions and conflict, providence and destiny,
being raised; but I would not try to determine for parents the point at
which the child, the growing boy or girl, should begin to move from one
world to the other.

All I can say is that to seek meaning, to examine critically, to
form one's own ideals and values, all such procedures in the school must
be introduced at the time appropriate, and it is the one who understands
the relationship of the two ways, that is, the teacher, who will know
when the time is appropriate. It is the teacher who will know when
pupils should be trained in debating, and when they should be taught the
difference between debating and making a judgment, who will know when
brave deeds may be allowed simply to speak for themselves and form the
pupil's ideals, and when the pupil should be led on to discuss whether
this or that heroic action, so obviously approved by the book and its

editor, is really worthwhile or not.   Allow me here another reminiscence. I was thrilling, at the age of twelve, to the poetry of war—
"Flash'd all their sabres bare," and all that—when our English teacher
brought in her clergyman to tell us what war had really been like in the
trenches from 1914 to 1918; the sabres never flashed in quite the same
way for me after that.

Carrying ideals into action is a further and very significant
step, in which teacher, counselor, clergyman, parent, have the delicate
task of balancing needed help against undue intervention in the pupil's
decisions. It does seem to me ridiculous for a three-year-old child to
decide whether to go on a weekend trip with its parents or stay at home
with friends, but I also see the need to allow the young to make
decisions themselves when parents would undoubtedly make better ones in
their stead. As I argued in chapter two, minor mistakes at ten years of
age may prevent major ones at twenty, and the only point to be added
here is the help an educator may give the ten-year-old in making capital
of a mistake—obviously, "I told you so" is not going to be the best
form of help. In all this delicate business I do not know of a better
goal for the educator to aim at than the role of the retreat director in
the Spiritual Exercises of Ignatius; that role is simply to stand aside
in the actual decision of retreatants, leaving them to work out their
choices in response to the movement of the Holy Spirit. Similarly, the
educator must eventually cease to intervene in any way that will determine the pupil's choices. As for a retreat of election, which I earlier
suggested for the decisive transitional period of a pupil's life, the
counseling educator might indeed play the extremely important role of
helping the young person decide if this is the time for such a retreat,
but within the Spiritual Exercises themselves, the counselor will yield
place to the Counselor who is the Holy Spirit.

Is such general advice on a flexible schedule of operations going
to help the educator very much?   I am sure that interpretation of it
will tend to move toward some polarization. The "progressive" educator
will begin much earlier to regard a poem as data, as material for stimulating ideas, provoking discussions, forming values, taking a position—
in short, for teaching pupils to think, judge, and decide for themselves.   The "traditional" teacher, on the contrary, will continue
longer to regard the poem as communicating the patrimony of the community, in the form either of sheer beauty, or of embodied values and

judgments, a way of life received as heritage from our ancestors. Without deciding between them, I cannot resist pointing out again that both these teachers are in fact communicating values and judgments, the progressive teacher by the choice of method, and the traditional teacher by the choice of a method as well as by the content of the poem.

My point, throughout this section, has been that it is the teacher who is the real agent, if there be one, in the integration of the way of heritage with the way of achievement, just as the teacher can be a powerful influence for disintegration, or for the lopsided stress on one way to neglect of the other. No matter what the directors of the school system, in capital city and government offices, decide to put into the school books, it is the teacher who, by approval or disapproval, expressed in words or conveyed in manner, most effectively forms the malleable child in the classroom. And, besides attitude toward poem or story, there is also praise or blame of the pupil's performance. I have already spoken in favor both of encouraging the child's ideas and rebuking its wrongdoing (a most effective means of communicating values, but rather gone out of fashion), but the powerful underlying influence of non-verbal communication should not be overlooked. In Newman's phrase, cor ad cor loquitur: heart speaks to heart. Or, to reinstate an old virtue, there is the power of good example, recorded for all time by Augustine in Book VIII of his Confessions, where he tells of those who rose up and took the kingdom of God by storm while he shillied and shallied, to capitulate at last and follow their example.

There is no need to multiply examples of an influence that hardly anyone will deny. But I do wish to make an application of some moment in community affairs. In the city where I live—and more widely too, I am sure—there is ever and again a hue and cry over the dismissal of a teacher for conduct in personal life that is said to be unbecoming or scandalous or in some way detrimental to the school system. The hue and cry, on the part of the teacher's critics, is some variation of the ancient charge of corrupting youth. On the other side, that of the teacher's defenders, it is a matter of human rights and the irrelevance of conduct outside the classroom to competence within the classroom: there is said to be no more ground here for dismissal than for firing a football player who has divorced his wife. Our analysis of the two ways of development throws a clearer light on such controversy and allows us to make pertinent distinctions. If the educational movement in the

school is predominantly a matter of development from below upward, as it
might well be in, say, a school for teaching auto mechanics their trade,
then the teacher's personal conduct outside the classroom is of lesser
moment. But, if the movement is still very much from above downward,
and especially in those stages where heart speaks more eloquently to
heart, as is the case when the school is forming young citizens, then
what the teacher is and does has much greater relevance to work in the
school, for we are in a situation where communication starts on the
basis of trust, to go through values and judgments, and so to seek
understanding.

One last word under this heading. It is prompted by the chaos of
our times, its rapid changes, the present urgency of the need to help
the young before they do something tragic with their lives. What I mean
is, that the school system, the books provided, the poems and stories,
could once upon a time be designed with a certain assurance that they
would suit the times, for the times changed slowly. I do not know what
the modern books have, for example, to prepare youth for their world of
drugs, violence, pornography, drifting institutions, that might compare
with the way books in my time prepared youth for the Protestant work
ethic, for bravery in battle, for loyalty to flag and country. I know
that progressive teachers hold endless classroom discussions on these
matters. And, so far as these discussions are effective in forming
judgments and values, more power to them.   But I am concerned with
invoking the great power of tradition (supposing that the value of this
has been given to the pupil), and the question then is, What are the
poems, stories, instances, histories, that will give the young an
embodied ideal today, that will portray a hero and heroine for the
"wingless youth" of our time,[15] something to capture their loyalty while
as yet their minds and hearts are too little molded, too volatile, too
unacquainted with life, either to form a real apprehension of their
world based on experience, or to create a personal value system that
arises out of the context through intelligence, reasonableness and
responsibility? My point is that we cannot be simply passive receivers

---

15. The quoted phrase is from an article by John W. Donohue, "Wingless
    Youth: Looking for Adolescence," _America_ 146 (April 10, 1982), pp.
    273-275.

of a tradition from the past, least of all in an age like ours; we have
also to be creative agents of a new and improved tradition, one that
operates on the level of the times.

4. Appended Note

The theme of this chapter has been the unification of the pupil's
development, the focus has been on the integration of the ways of
achievement and heritage, and the structuring idea has been that of the
levels of consciousness. But there are few or no subjective operations
without an object; there is no exercise of experience, understanding,
judgment, and deliberation, without something experienced, understood,
affirmed or denied, chosen or not chosen. There is no method of schooling without the reading of some books or other, studying the history and
geography of some land or other, and the rest.

Now in the content of what is taught, there is ample room for
profoundly differing judgments and values that may divide pupil from
pupil or even divide the individual pupil interiorly. Such inner
division is much more likely to have its source on the side of tradition. Our own achievements, just because they are our own, will tend to
insert themselves into our already established "system" and become one
with it. But traditions are various; for example, those brought from
home may differ from those contained in the school books. I mentioned
the difficulty for a Catholic boy of Irish ancestry whose schooling
included a large dose of British and Protestant judgments and values.
Here then is the problem (I state it as mine, but anyone may generalize
my statement): I am not engaged merely in becoming myself as an individual human being, that is, Fred Crowe, with his experience, understanding, judgment, values; my problem is to become myself in my part of
a divided world, that is, Fred Crowe who, by lot or by choice, happens
also to be a Canadian, a Christian and a Roman Catholic, living in the
First or Western world, and so on.

Let me pursue my particular case along lines that are not so
readily generalizable, for that too will contribute to our perspective.
The particular Canadian experience, then, from the viewpoint of this
chapter, is quite different from the British or the American. I am not
thinking of our bilingual situation; that is another, though related,

problem. My point is rather that the British identity grew over a
period of a thousand and more years, the American identity was forged
rapidly in a Declaration of Independence and a Revolutionary War, and
the Canadian experience is neither one of these. In terms of growing an
identity, we are about where the British were in the late Middle Ages
with the emergence of European nationalism; in terms of independence, we
reached with our Constitution of 1982, and then rather half-heartedly, a
point the Americans reached in 1776 or maybe 1783. One may well wonder
how a Canadian identity emerged at all, to the extent that it did; and
some may wonder whether it can survive for, replacing the British emphasis found in our early school books, is the almost overwhelming influence of American culture carried across our borders in the media
explosion. If we survive—I know of no decree of Providence guaran-
teeing this, and we have no destiny that is manifest to me—but if we
survive, as in love and loyalty we struggle to do, we may have done
something close to being unique in national identity-formation: becoming
ourselves without being anti anyone else.

   Three remarks may bring us back from this personal illustration
to topics of general interest to educators. First, the question of
diverse influences in forming national self-identity reminds us again of
the need to relate the school to the variety of less formal educational
influences coming from other sources: from home and church, from radio,
cinema and television, from press and public library, from museum and
art gallery, from circus and baseball diamond, especially from national
self-government and the fever of elections, and always from people, be
they neighbors, teammates, employers, whoever. Ivan Illich is so sensitive to these influences that he would go to the opposite extreme from
over-zealous educators and simply "deschool" society.[16]   But this,
understandable though it be in a man without a country, simply contra-
dicts the experience of too many of us to be acceptable: the literature
and history we learned in our school books, even when they created
tensions for minorities, have left too deep an impression.

   That leads to my second remark. While national self-identity is
likely to remain with us a long time, and education is bound to contribute to its development, the era of nationalism so intense as to verge
on chauvinism is coming to an end. Older nations have to learn this

16. Ivan Illich, Deschooling Society (New York: Harper & Row, 1970,
    1971).

lesson in bitter repentance; younger nations have to give up nationalist ambitions just when they might have been realized. But what will we introduce into our schooling to be the world counterpart of the national factor, to promote our human self-identity as that of members of a global village? Must we not have a literature, a history, a set of school books, that take our planet more consciously as our home, our context for life? Must not the judgments and values that are handed on or achieved, point the way to greater collaboration among nations, whether it be to build a Concorde or feed a famished people?

And so to my third remark, which returns to the subjective side in order to suggest a wider application of the transcendental precepts: be attentive, be intelligent, be reasonable, be responsible. For these continue to work even when the objective situation is otherwise completely absurd and utterly hopeless. If there is no way two boys can eat the same piece of cake, or find principles of justice by which to divide it equitably, there is a way to the attention, intelligence, reasonableness, and responsibility of each. God knows we have enough absurd situations among the nations, made more and more hopeless by conflicting appeals to justice. But, where justice is objective and may reach an impasse, responsibility is subjective and is never brought to an impasse. Can nations learn this? If educators have any part in the forming of citizens, their responsibility is clear.[17]

---

17. I have taken formation of citizens merely as an example, but the principle applies more widely. For example, if we are to speak of the responsibilities of educators in regard to the civic traditions of a people, we should also speak of a parallel responsibility in regard to the religious traditions of a family, a people, a church; these are as much a part of our patrimony as democracy is, and one of which the young are too often deprived. There is an air of unreality, not to say injustice, in a parental decision to tell children nothing of things religious till they can decide for themselves on reaching, say, their teens—by which time they will be so deep into important matters like basketball and class debates that they cannot be bothered with a treasure which anyway a whole secular culture will have meanwhile taught them to despise. Of course, one can plead freedom of conscience, but I do not know of any parents who keep their child in ignorance of our national history or our democratic way of life, in order that there be freedom of conscience to choose between the Russian way and ours when teenage comes along.

CHAPTER FIVE

POST-SECONDARY EDUCATION

The relationship of the two ways of development has been clarified, I think, by express attention to the adolescent period of rebellion. The fact that two quite different forces have been at work in the
pupil becomes clear when we see the two paths cross and the two forces
enter into conflict: growing self-reliance on the part of the pupil;
reluctant relinquishing of control, and perhaps a last-ditch effort to
maintain it, on the part of the elders. The victory, however, is fore-
ordained: it goes to the young with their star in the ascendant. They
have developed in many ways: biological, psychic, social; they are
attaining the physical stature of an adult, sex characteristics are
emerging, the psyche changing; they form friendships instead of finding
chums (one brings one's "chums" home at the age of ten, one goes out
with one's "friends" at the age of eighteen). The effort of elders to
retain the importance they had when their children were young (how deep
is the need we all have to be "important" and how easily in a parent it
fixes on the importance to his or her children), is almost as futile as
the effort to resist old age and death.

For some guidance through this difficult transition we formed an
ideal type of the final product and described some general goals at
which we might aim. Now, of course, no goals are final; all life is
transition. Still, the transition is not just an even flow, perpetual
flux without variation. There are stages and plateaus that divide and
mark the journey. One of these is pretty clearly the stage we will call
university education, and that will be the main topic in this chapter.
My plan: to study the path in university studies of experience, understanding, reflection, and values, concentrating rather on the humanities
than on the natural sciences; then to study the ways in which the path
of values, reflection, understanding, and experience is still operative;
thirdly, to examine the nature of the doctoral dissertation which marks

the term of formal education, the "commencement" of life for real; and,
finally, to add some remarks on   aspects   of "real life" that seem more
pertinent to our two ways of development.

1. The Way of Achievement in the University

Our students, on leaving secondary education to enter university,
have mastered a good many skills that go far beyond the reading, writing
and arithmetic of the primary grades.   They know something of reasoning
processes, and can debate and argue many a question.   They can likewise
compose a respectable essay, and use the ordinary tools and library
resources available for quick   information.   They have been through a
selection of literature, and are acquainted with a number of characters
in classical poetry, drama and fiction.   They have studied an outline of
world history and world geography, and   are aware of the varieties in
family customs, styles of government, and other cultural forms among the
peoples of the globe. They have been taught something of a number of
sciences, mainly in a descriptive way, and have begun the advanced
mathematics by which to master them later in explanatory understanding.
The new experiences of puberty, some involvement in local politics, a
certain amount of travel, will have broadened the basis for real apprehension of human affairs as contrasted with notional. In short, the
student seems to be about ready for a more decisive shift from the way
of tradition to the way of achievement.
    Now, if this transition is not to be simply an even flow, a
matter of imperceptible degrees of difference, subject only to that
understanding that differential calculus might provide, but is to be
marked by determinate stages, then there has to be something like a
qualitative difference in those successive stages. I believe there are
such differences between pre-adolescent and post-adolescent years; I
think also that our system of secondary and post-secondary education
reveals them with a certain clarity, and so I will speak in this chapter
of the character of university education, while deferring to educators
themselves for the exact location of the stages on a time-scale in the
student's life.
    What I am saying is that the series, experience-understanding-
reflection-values, is an analogous concept.   It is partly the same

whether the subject be in primary grades or university, but it is partly different. I am saying further that the difference is not just a matter of the pattern, experience-understanding-reflection-values, being more prominent in later years in comparison with its counterpart, the pattern that starts with values; I am saying that there are significant differences within the functioning of that first pattern itself as a dynamism, and it is those differences that concern us now. I should say that, in primary and perhaps still more in secondary education, experience-understanding-reflection-values functioned to effect the unfolding of the four levels as distinct levels. The focus of attention was not therefore the content (though this had to be a concern of the educator, following the dynamism of the opposite route, based on values), but rather the activity itself as distinctive of each level, and the expression given the activity in the tools and media of human communication. But in the university, though one continues the appropriation of the four levels (and does so to the end of life), attention is turned rather to the materials on which they are exercised, and to the results of their accurate use and application. That difference will be indicated in this chapter by use of the series, research, interpretation, history, and dialectic, rather than of experience, understanding, reflection, and values. This latter foursome applies to the whole of life; it regards the common element in the analogous concept I spoke of. But the other foursome belongs to the specialized world of the university; it regards the element of difference in the analogous concept. This general assertion has now to be studied in more detail.

a. On the first level then, the shift will be from a rather haphazard collecting and storing of experience to the research and assembly of data for a particular question of scholarship. That is, in kindergarten and in much of primary school, the child accumulates experience at a rapid rate. But it simply accumulates; it is taken into the mind as into a receptacle; it is not organized, or oriented toward understanding in a fully conscious way. I have used some of Newman's terms; let me quote him more at length.

> Memory is one of the first developed of the mental faculties; a
> boy's business when he goes to school is to learn, that is, to
> store up things in his memory. For some years his intellect is
> little more than an instrument for taking in facts, or a recep-

tacle for storing them; he welcomes them as fast as they come to
him; he lives on what is without; he has his eyes ever about
him; he has a lively susceptibility of impressions; he imbibes
information of every kind; and little does he make his own in a
true sense of the word, living rather upon his neighbours all
around him ... Geography, chronology, history, language, natural
history, he heaps up the matter of these studies as treasures
for a future day.[1]

What keeps this process from being merely the stocking of a warehouse with
goods of the mind (or filling a wastepaper basket with junk)? It is, on
one side, the dynamism of the pupil's consciousness which cannot be forever
satisfied with chaos, and, on the other, the care with which elders both
guide the accumulation of experience in the young and orient the exercise
of their built-in dynamism. But only slowly does the process go forward
till the jump to a qualitative difference becomes possible. Even in high
school, the young are busier with fictional figures than with historical;
they know the character of Hamlet better than that of Oliver Cromwell.
Their history and geography show overall views rather than a scholar's
mastery. But in university there is a definite transition: now they
research data; that is, they go looking for them, and that in regard to
very specific questions. They are not satisfied with a general view of
history, or with the isolated fact that Columbus discovered America in
1492: they want the antecedents and consequent unfolding of that bare fact,
some way of locating it in ongoing history with a real apprehension.

The transition on this first level is seen in the way of both
achievement and heritage. I spoke earlier, in regard to the former way, of
the difference among experience, data, and technical data. Perhaps those
three terms are clearer now: the child accumulates experience; the youth
begins to see experience as a basis for raising questions, that is, experience now becomes data for understanding; the researcher seeks out data,
classifies them, makes them a highly technical element in the ongoing work
of academe. At the same time, the way of heritage is affected by the
transition: briefly, materials are shifted from the syndrome of values,
reflection, understanding, and experience, to the opposite order. That is,
the nursery rhymes, poems, stories that accumulated in the child's experience, also conveyed to it values, judgments, meanings. Now those same
rhymes, poems, stories, become for the university student data for interpretation and history—and for dialectic too, insofar as one begins to

1. Newman, The Idea of a University, pp. 127-28.

examine the horizons of those involved and take a position in regard to the truths they held and the values they treasured. It is not that the data have lost their meaning, their intention of conveying values and judgments, but that the meaning is not received without examination, the judgment accepted without critique, the value made one's own without deliberation. The data remain what they were, but the attitude of the subject is different: what for the child was the mysterious noise of thunder becomes for the university student an observable phenomenon to be measured in decibels.

b. There is a corresponding shift in the functioning of understanding as one moves into university studies. The early years of school are given over to an understanding of words, for language is the basic tool of academic communication and of much of human living. One works painfully to acquire the art of expression, to develop in some small measure a "style" of writing. At some point, perhaps in the high school years, one turns through literature to an understanding of human nature; this is mainly sought, however, through ideal types, or through figures of fiction, one's own experience being as yet insufficient to bear the weight of accurate knowledge of, and judgment in, human affairs. But in university the effort is not scientia nominis but scientia rei, not notional but real apprehension, not debate in play but discussion in earnest. The shift toward understanding of real objects is accompanied or followed by another, the shift from the descriptive, which is largely a matter of knowing the meaning of words, to the explanatory, which is much more a matter of relation of part to part and of each to the whole, of understanding systematically those things to which the words refer.[2]

Thus, to illustrate the point about composition, I remember being once assigned a paragraph of Newman for imitation, and proceeding to describe St. Peter's in Rome as an imperturbable old cathedral on the banks of the Tiber, very satisfied with my phrase and quite unconcerned with the realities: whether St. Peter's was a cathedral, or even on the banks of the Tiber. I likewise remember that in high school we debated the characters of Brutus and Cassius, as dramatized in Julius Caesar; no doubt we were subjectively in deep earnest, but I would expect a university seminar to

---

2. See note 8 to chapter four, where a distinction is made between a pupil who studies words for scientia nominis, and a university professor who studies the same words for scientia rei.

discuss such a question with far more relevance to reality than we could
achieve in those early years.   The purpose now becomes, not composition or
debate, but understanding of the world that exists, the one disclosed by
physics, chemistry, biology, and the other sciences, as well as the world
of the arts, the world of politics, the world of daily living, etc. And in
the human world the purpose is not merely a knowledge of human nature
through typical figures of literature, but the knowledge proper either to
scholarship or to the human sciences: in scholarship, the study of the
particular meaning of a particular author, or the particular course of a
particular movement; in the human sciences, the explanatory laws of human
conduct. So that, as there was a transition from experience through data
to data brought under technical control on the first level, there is now on
the second level a transition from understanding language, through debating
questions in an ideal way, to the serious discussions that lead to the
understanding proper to science and scholarship.

      This development is very apt to have one unfortunate effect: a real
narrowing of outlook. One student goes into nuclear physics, another into
medieval history, and a third into modern literature. There is specialization both in subject matter and in field, in subject matter according to
categories (biology, zoology, and the many -ologies), in field according to
the divisions of space and time (the history of the Western front from ten
to eleven on the morning of November 11, 1918). But this can be countered
by the general view on God, man, and the universe, provided by philosophy
and theology. And to keep this from becoming still another mere specialty,
or various specialties, each of unmanageable detail,[3] there is the transcendental approach and the generalized empirical method which is radically
applicable in all human endeavor.   This topic, one of considerable importance, will recur later when we come to the question of interdisciplinary
studies.

      c. If the university student is concerned to understand the real
world and not some ideal one of fancy or of fiction, it remains that understanding of the real is not yet knowledge of the real. So we come now to

---

3. Philosophy and theology are specializations too, by reason of their
   specialized languages and so on; but they are general insofar as
   philosophy sublates other sciences and theology sublates philosophy.
   (Sublation does not mean interference in the proper work of the
   sublated science.)

that third level, and have to study a corresponding shift, when one moves
from lower to higher studies, in the cognitional operation that we call
knowledge, judgment, or affirmation of what is. In the pupil's early
years, as we saw, judgments are supplied largely by some form of tradition,
either current tradition or heritage from the past. As Newman remarked
(quotation above), a boy's mind lives on his neighbors all round him. If
this tradition did not always take the form of explicit propositions, there
was still a set of values that would issue in explicit views as occasion
demanded. But efforts toward personal judgment were bound to be ineffec-
tual,‑limited to the sort of logical or rhetorical thinking that might
enter into a debate or a literary composition, "thinking" here being taken
in distinction from "knowing," and understood as a step on the way to
knowing. The focal development was, therefore, in the act and activity of
judgment; such assents as the young were able to give to a proposition
were, like their apprehension of realities, notional assents.[4] But in
university the focal interest is in the content of judgments; the main
concern is with the materials to be judged, and not with the form in which
one expresses one's judgments. A concrete instance: one studies the Battle
of Agincourt, not to appropriate the brave tradition of one's ancestors,
but to learn what factors could account for the victory of so few over so
many. Another: in engineering one's concern is not with getting the
abstract answer of a book-problem, with its magic accuracy, but in determining what to do in concrete reality; for example, a high school answer in
the mechanics book might be that this beam will bear a weight of 16,873.5
pounds, where the engineer would say that it will bear around 15,000
pounds, and, to ensure safety, would set the maximum load in practise at
5,000 pounds.

A feature of judgment is the exercise of the critical capacity, not
in the sense of praise or blame—that belongs to the fourth level—but in
the sense of examining propositions for their truth, checking one's assump-
tions for their validity, and the like. This exercise will have been
taught the growing student, that is, handed over as part of his or her
heritage, as tradition. In the developmental process we are describing,

---

4. The young learn to deal with propositions, as the church learned to
   deal with revelation formulated in propositions at the council of
   Nicea and afterward; they do not know this, but neither do they know
   they are speaking prose.

where the pupil moves from reliance on others to self-reliance, there is
not the slightest contradiction in teaching the pupil not to accept the
teaching uncritically. (There is a contradiction in the practise of extremists who are against all tradition, but hand over to the pupil their
thinking, their judgments, their decisions, which is that the pupil, think,
judge, decide for himself or herself; but we need not labor that point
again.) The only question at the moment, then, is whether there is a significant transition when the youth moves to criticism at the university
level. My suggestion is that, where earlier pupils were taught to critique
their own judgment, with the emphasis then on the activity, now at university they will learn to critique what is proffered as true, with the emphasis then on the content of the judgment. Of course, this means critiquing
the whole of tradition from the past, all that they have been taught,
including the tradition that taught them to critique tradition, but going
on naturally to critique the statements of contemporaries, the pronounce-
ments of historians, still more those of statesmen, and most sharply of
all, those of politicians.

     d. We come to the fourth level, and to an oddity in the set of
transitions we are trying to describe in the university student. For I
suggested that within the third level, the transition is from a critique of
one's own judging activity to a critique of the objective judgments offered
one for assent. But that very application of third-level critical capacity
to the tradition will have the effect on the fourth level of turning one
back to a critique of one's own subjective state again. For the critique
of tradition, and especially any tradition in human studies and human
sciences, will raise sooner or later, or should raise sooner or later, the
question of who it is that offers the critique, what the horizon of interests and concerns within which it is offered, how authentically attention,
intelligence, reflection and deliberation are exercised in offering it.
     Immensely helpful here are Lonergan's analyses of interpretation,
history, and dialectic. The analysis was initiated in Insight, in the
discussion of truth in the chapter on interpretation.

     The subject becomes more or less secure or anxious about the
     genuineness of his inquiry and reflection, and further inquiry
     and reflection will in their turn be open to similar questioning.

What is in doubt is the subject himself, and all his efforts to
remove the doubt will proceed from the same suspected source.[5]

This analysis is greatly amplified in his Method in Theology, with its
separate chapters on research, interpretation, and history, leading up
to the critical evaluation of the human subject in the chapter on dialectic.[6] The historian, the interpreter, and the researcher too, is
always a human subject, and it is always the human subject who comes
eventually into question, for we work within a consciousness that has a
horizon, are exposed to the danger that a too narrow horizon has pre-
vented us from assembling the data that should be examined, from understanding what should be understood, from asserting what should be
asserted. A university student is nowhere near the pinnacle of authenticity that would give immunity to bias. But I am suggesting that the
student is now in a position to tackle the problem where in earlier
years he or she would hardly even advert to it. It is a matter once
again of the need for the slow passing of the years and the gradual
development of experience, understanding, and judgment—this time in
regard especially to oneself and the critical evaluation of one's own
horizons.

There are other factors, less radical but more likely to impinge
on the consciousness, that will affect the fourth-level activity of
university students. Many "real-life" decisions begin to press upon
them: short-range problems, like that of financing their university
studies; longer-range problems such as marriage now or later, perhaps
the choice of a career itself. If they have made a choice in these
longer-range matters, there will be particular questions on the views
and ethics that pertain to the consequences of the choice. Then in a
university there will be a tradition of student activism (itself a sign
of the new "realism" marking the transition on all four levels at this
time), and one must take a stand in regard both to what the activists
advocate and to one's own role in such activism. Further, being a
citizen, of voting age or near it, one must take a position, at home or

---

5. Lonergan, Insight, p. 551.

6. Lonergan, Method, chapters 6, 7, 8, and 10. The succinct answer of
   Method to the problem raised in Insight is: "Genuine objectivity is
   the fruit of authentic subjectivity" (p. 292; see also pp. 265, 338).

on campus, on civic and national questions.   And so on. But since I
will refer soon to two samples of "real life" that are especially relevant to the four levels, perhaps   I   may omit further discussion of such
questions here.

2. University Education as Shared Heritage

I have been characterizing the way of human achievement in the
university student, taking the constants as an assumed basis, and
studying the variations in the form they might take at this stage. My
suggestion has been that the generic and constant basis of experience,
understanding, reflection, values is specified now in the form of
research, interpretation, history and dialectic—recognizing that these
categories apply to the humanities with a special appropriateness. But
human development is never just achievement, not after the first man and
woman anyway, just as life itself is never just achievement. From
beginning to end of life there is heritage, tradition, gift, and from
beginning to end of education there is similarly a role for that way of
heritage which we have found to be complementary to the way of achievement from kindergarten onward.

But tradition too is an analogous concept and, just as we found
the constants of achievement taking on a special form proper to the
university, so in the way of heritage there is a constant basis found in
both child and researcher, but there is a particular form too that this
way takes in the latter. Constant is the role of receiving in trust, a
role found in the university researcher as well as in the child. But
there is specific variation in the advanced student which I have tried
to indicate by calling this section, University Education as Shared
Heritage. The specific word is obviously "shared," and I hope to make
its significance somewhat clearer in the following paragraphs. Three
subheadings occur to me as especially germane to the topic: the role of
the first four specialties as mediating the personal stance of the
student; next, the role of interdisciplinary studies in a university;
and, thirdly, the role of a specifically Christian university in
academe.

a. My first point is that research, interpretation, history, and dialectic, though they have a value in themselves, though they may in fact preoccupy students or professors for long years without leading to further involvement on their part, are nevertheless by their nature tributary to the personal stance, doctrine, guiding system, involvement with one's fellows, that belong to the student as a person. And it is worth reminding ourselves of the student's need to remain a person, of the danger indeed of ceasing in some sense to be a person when preoccupied in academe. As the epitaph said, "Born John Jones, child of Adam and Martha Jones. Died, a university professor."

Lonergan's field is method in theology, and his concern the union of tradition and innovation in theological questions, but he asserts that the same pattern holds for any field of human studies that investigate a cultural past to guide its future. If he is correct, his application to theology will serve to illustrate for us a wider use. Let us see how that works out. There are, then, two phases of theology. One is mediating: research, interpretation, history, dialectic. It is mediating in the sense that through study of the past I may come to a position of my own in the present. But in itself, it is theology in oratione obliqua: what Paul said, what was happening at Nicea, and the like. The second phase is mediated theology: my theology, what I hold and understand and teach. The terms, mediating and mediated, suggest the close relationship of the two phases; they are not alternatives but a unit, they need and complement one another. My mediated theology is the transposition of the mediating theology of the past, a theology that has been put through the crucible of dialectic and restated in categories that derive from interiority, a theology then that is meaningful to me as the original theology was meaningful to its exponents.

Now, mutatis mutandis, the same can be said of human studies in general in the university. There is a mediating and a mediated phase; the past is not just junk to be jettisoned, and the new is not a creation ex nihilo, but a transposition of a purified past. Let research be ever so meticulous, let interpretation take the fullest account of the time-conditioned character of ancient documents, let history record all the vicissitudes and transitions of my community, lay bare the past with all its warts and cancers, let dialectic reveal in the most embarrassing detail the biases of my ancestors—there is still

a legacy, else we would not claim any community with our ancestors, or
show any interest in their literary remains and other bequests.

Now I wish to set all this in relation to the youth who is
entering university. I do not ask whether or to what extent the university itself in a secular and pluralist society can or should accept,
declare and promote a particular set of values and views, in responsibility to the community, the nation, the world family—these are large
questions, larger than I contracted to handle in this book. I do assume
that individual professors will have a degree of liberty for second-
phase self-involvement and not be restricted to research, interpretation, history, and dialectic. And happy will be the student who finds
such a professor to be his guide, philosopher, and friend to help him
through these years.

It is the students, of course, who are the focus of our interest.
And our question is, What relevance has the way of heritage for them now
in the new and complex situation where they are freed from the domination of elders in their choice of values, their judgments on the universe, the meaning they find in life, and their selection of resources
from the immense hopper of materials before them? I think that we can
see now the importance of that graduated and carefully managed transition from a position of dependence to one of independence that we spoke
of in chapter four.   If the transition has been initiated and carried
forward without disaster in secondary education, the student will have
learned the way of achievement, and done so quite thoroughly, without
any need to abandon wholesale the way of tradition; he or she will have
come to appreciate the way of tradition—that will have been one of his
or her achievements. It is this development that will stand one in good
stead now that one is in a much greater degree on one's own, set free in
the garden of intellectual delights, able to roam at will in the various
provinces of intellect, to examine every idea, movement, system, and the
crop of new isms that grow like weeds with every generation.

Secondly, the student is not without external help from the past
itself. There is an innate power in its literary remains, in the
history of its great deeds.   The classics would not have come down to
us, nor would they be studied today, if they were not truly classics.
Thus, they will exercise their own attraction for mind and heart, their
own power to form ideals, to direct judgment, to give life a meaning.
It is hard to imagine a student making a career of studying Shakespeare

and not continuing to learn from Shakespeare a great deal about human nature. Or making a career of studying Cicero and not learning from Cicero what beautiful things can be done with language. Or encountering Augustine's Confessions and not feeling challenged in one's own personal life decisions. The one supposition here is, of course, that Shakespeare, Cicero, Augustine may still be studied. But surely one may safely rely for this on the university as university, for by profession it is the seat of universal learning. Whether these three authors will find professors to teach them is a question, but one hopes that this is one small area in which the individual professor may still exercise an individual choice, and be a hander-on of tradition.

There is a third factor that is simply the second brought into sharper focus. A university career ends for the student, as one of the student class, with the doctoral dissertation. A doctoral dissertation in human studies is commonly, and rightly, a study of some great figure from the past. It can hardly be that a student who is open to the two ways of development will spend months and years of diligent research into and study of the works of one of the greats from the past, and not be humbly and profoundly transformed; if indeed one is not so transformed, then I would say that one has made a poor choice of topic for the dissertation. But of that more particularly in my fourth section in this chapter.

b. I have argued that a university student is by no means cut altogether loose from tradition and wholly dedicated to new achievement. Research, interpretation, and history reveal treasures that will not be ignored, their power and attraction being what they are. When all that is obsolete has been discarded, and all that is corrupt has been purified, there remains a heritage to be developed and transposed. All this seems so simple and obvious that it might well have gone without saying, did not extremist opposition to tradition impose on us a statement of the obvious.

But now I wish to make a second and less obvious point. Besides our relation to the past and dependence on our ancestors, there is also our relation to the present and dependence on our contemporary workers in the great web of disciplines that constitute the program of a university. This, the theme on almost every page of Newman's nine lectures on

The Idea of a University, is stated with special clarity near the
beginning of Discourse V.

> I have said that all branches of knowledge are connected
> together, because the subject-matter of knowledge is intimately
> united in itself, as being the acts and the work of the Creator.
> Hence it is that the Sciences, into which our knowledge may be
> said to be cast, have multiplied bearings one on another, and an
> internal sympathy, and admit, or rather demand, comparison and
> adjustment. They complete, correct, balance each other.[7]

Now Newman makes his point here a priori: there must be a web of
sciences, because they all study the work of one Creator. The point is
valid enough in regard to the fact, but does not tell us much about the
actual fabric of that web: how do we relate the sciences, hold them
together in unity? what principle is there, if any, internal to the
sciences themselves, that grounds "their multiplied bearings one on
another"? Newman's own work was a pretty sustained effort to answer
that question, so he would not dispute the need of going beyond the
lines I quoted. How are we to go beyond them? My own position is that
the medieval way of Thomist wisdom is not possible in this age of
specialization, that the renaissance way of the uomo universale is only
a dream now, but that the modern way of interdisciplinary procedures can
effect an advance on Newman in the direction he desired us to go.
Still, the interdisciplinary way is itself in need of a foundation, and
this I think is supplied by the structures of consciousness that have
been our constants all along. Finally, I think that such interdisciplinary cooperation belongs in its own way to development from above,
and is analogous to our way of heritage, of tradition. That is the main
point of the title "shared heritage" and must be explained now in somewhat more detail.

For Aquinas, then, wisdom was the overarching factor in
knowledge. It was wisdom that chose the terms for first principles,
that governed the derivation of conclusions from those principles, that
settled the most universal notion of all, the notion of being. Wisdom's
instrument was metaphysics, which entered into the lesser sciences as a
premise, and so was the unifying force for all of them. This short

---

7. Newman, Idea of a University, p. 99.

sketch relies on Lonergan, whose early work laid heavy stress on wisdom.[8]
But Lonergan came to see the need of distinguishing a more open view of
Thomist wisdom from one that was too intertwined with the notion of
science attributed to Aristotle. In that view, science pertained to the
timeless and necessary realm, where certainty was queen and the universal was king, where change was banished to the margins, and conclusions
could be demonstrated. Today, metaphysics does not serve as the unifying factor for the sciences, and science itself is not demonstrated;
further it is the possession, not of any single scientist, but of the
scientific community; it is "shared," parceled out among the community
members. And so the term, wisdom, used in the sense we meet in
Lonergan's study of Aquinas, almost disappears from his later works.[9]

The universal man of the Italian Renaissance was not at all the
Thomist type. He would combine comprehensive learning with one or more
of the arts or professions. His academic ideal was humanism and a
general education, with mathematics often the organon of the undertaking. He was the product of the "orderly, practical, and confident
urban world" of fourteenth- and fifteenth-century Italy. When that
world collapsed, the type disappeared, and the very notion of universal
man became discredited. Leonardo da Vinci is said to be an outstanding
exemplar, but already in him there is a separation of humanism from the
artistic-technical current. And Michelangelo, the most universal artist
of them all, represents the further separation of art from scientific
preoccupations. In him and his history, in fact, we can see the "final
dissolution" of the Renaissance dream: "Art, science and literary
humanism henceforth pursued their own independent careers." The univer-

8. See the index to Verbum under "Wisdom." This stress continues in the
   post-Insight period, being found, for example, in De intellectu et
   methodo (1959; see esp. pp. 17-22).

9. Consult the indices to Method, A Second Collection, etc.; again under
   "Wisdom." On knowledge as parceled out in a community of scientists,
   see A Second Collection, p. 51 (in "The Future of Thomism") and p.
   140 (in "Theology and Man's Future").

sal man, we may say, was fragmented into specializations.[10]

So we come to interdisciplinary studies which themselves, however, need a common basis; otherwise we continue the dialogue of the
deaf. The basis is not a common field, for that has been divided and
subdivided beyond calculation. The basis is not some overarching
concept, which is likely to be abstract and in any case will not be
accepted by all participants. The basis will have to be in the
thinking, knowing subject, in the operations by which the subject moves
from level to level of consciousness, in the stages which are united one
to another as differentiations of one and the same specific consciousness in different subjects. Researcher, interpreter, historian, apologist, and theologian can talk to one another about the same document if
they agree that data must be assembled, understood, located in history,
allowed to challenge us personally. Further, biblicist, patristic
scholar, medievalist can talk about the same idea or doctrine or
treatise or division of church teaching, if they agree on basic differentiations of human consciousness and consequent stages of meaning.

All that is very rapidly said, for it is not the focal point of
my remarks. The focus for me here is the fact that in interdisciplinary
studies we are committing ourselves in a new way to tradition. As we
accept the testimony of the apostles on matters we can no longer observe
for ourselves, so we accept the collaboration of other disciplines in
matters whose study we cannot in this age of specialization undertake
for ourselves. Thus, while work within any particular discipline may be
largely work in the way of achievement, the sharing, the mutual giving

---

10. For this paragraph on the universal man of the Renaissance I have
    relied entirely on Joan Kelly Gadol, "Universal Man," Dictionary of
    the History of Ideas, edited by P. P. Wiener (New York: Scribner's,
    1973), 4:437-443. For the quoted phrases, see pp. 441-442 and 443.
       The general idea of this subsection (the sequence from Thomist
    wisdom through the Renaissance uomo universale to modern interdisci-
    plinary cooperation) was worked out in a paper I prepared for a
    workshop on "Bernard Lonergan's Interdisciplinary Philosophy,"
    organized by Prof. Philip McShane and held at Mount Saint Vincent's
    University, Halifax, Nova Scotia, in October, 1975. I am much
    indebted to Prof. McShane for the stimulus of that workshop.

and receiving, which rest on belief and trust, are formally the kind of work that belongs in the way of tradition, of the human as gift.

c. I have omitted so far all mention of a Christian or Catholic university and what that means for the two ways of educational movement and process. It is not because of its lack of importance that I omitted it, for obviously it is of front-ranking importance. Rather is it because the whole idea needs special treatment, and that in a proper context. I reserve that question therefore to a later chapter, where it will appear in the context of a Christian view of education. For the moment, it will be enough to say that a university that calls itself Christian cannot be neutral to the Christian message: further, that the Christian message is given, but given as a talent to be developed, not buried in the ground. Consequently, there will necessarily be elements of both achievement and heritage in the Christian university. It is useful to note that inevitability in this chapter on the university student, while reserving explanation for another time.

3. The Doctoral Dissertation

As in some old-fashioned societies young ladies make their debut, and as ships are launched on a maiden voyage, so those who choose an academic career begin with a doctoral dissertation. It leads to their "commencement," as it is accurately called in the ceremonies of some universities. My interest, however, is not in the dissertation as start of a career, but as end of formal schooling, the last plateau on that long climb that began with kindergarten. If our structuring of the educational process has the universality I have claimed for it, it should apply here too.

The question, then, is how the dissertation, as a task in education, is illuminated by the two ways of tradition and achievement. And my own answer would offer a distinction. Formally, the work of doctoral candidates pertains more to the way of achievement: nowhere yet in their course of studies have they been left so much on their own, to do their own research, offer their own interpretation, write history as they see it, respond to the challenge as they encounter it. But materially their work is far more likely to be profitable if it is done in the way of

tradition, if they take the work of a master for study, instead of
setting forth their own independent thinking on the universe or on some
part of it. One will indeed make one's own statement and take one's own
stand, but in order to declare one's view on what it is that someone
else has said; it will be discourse in oratione obliqua, not in oratione
recta, a dissertation that studies, say, Anselm's views on redemption,
and does not offer a new theory of redemption to a waiting theological
world.

I suggest this pattern as the more likely to profit the candidate. This is my personal position on what a doctoral dissertation
should ordinarily be, confirmed for me by a certain amount of experience
in directing candidates, but originally based on an argument set forth
by Lonergan. He used to say, long before he had worked out his two
phases of theology, that the formula for a thesis is "What X says on Y."
His reasoning was simple. The alternatives are a study of someone
else's ideas, or an exposition of your own. If you devote two, three,
or more years to the exposition of your own idea, you may find in the
end that you didn't really have anything very significant to say when
you began and that, in any case, you have not advanced very far beyond
your beginning: one tends to spin out one's idea, gossamer-style, from
within, instead of having it challenged and maybe demolished from without. But, if you try the alternative and devote your doctoral investigation to the study of another, and that other a thinker of stature, not
only will you have something concrete and materially definite to present
(no gossamers here), but your own mind will have been stretched and
forced to grow in the encounter. And you may have opened up as well a
field for a lifelong career of study.

Everything in my experience confirms the wisdom of that advice,
considered as a general policy. Further, the need for giving the advice
recurs with remarkable regularity. I mean that students almost invariably come to doctoral work with an idea whose implications they hope to
explore and offer to the university world in their dissertation. More
power to their inventive minds. How would anything creative ever happen
in the intellectual world without such persons and their ideas? But,
just as invariably as I encounter such a candidate, I advise that the
great idea be put for the present on the back-burner, and I quote the
sentence from Insight we have already seen in part:

> The child would understand everything at once. It does not
> suspect that there is a strategy in the accumulation of in-
> sights, that the answers to many questions depend on answers to
> still other questions, that, often enough, advertence to these
> other questions arises only from the insight that to meet inter-
> esting questions one has to begin from quite uninteresting ones.[11]

I do not mean that I discourage the great idea—one will hardly perse-
vere through the grind of a doctorate without some such impetus—but I
suggest that the candidate could make a good start toward full treatment
of the idea, and at the same time finish the doctorate within the bud-
geted time, if he or she were to study the thinker, X, on the topic, Y,
"Y" being some small subdivision of the great idea.

Doctoral candidates, in my experience, are really fairly humble
people, grateful for the chance to do higher studies and willing to
listen to advice; they accept, then, readily enough (maybe even with a
certain relief) postponement of the great idea. But there remains the
choice of a specific topic. That is indeed half the battle, quite
literally half the battle in terms of time and energy and investigation.
An explorer may ascend many a valley, and sometimes climb rather high,
only to discover there is no pass that way through the mountains, that
he or she must descend and try another way. And a doctoral dissertation
is essentially an exploration.

Still, all exploration will use whatever help is already available, and in the intellectual exploration of the dissertation, categories are available to guide the procedures of the candidate. If the
thesis is to be a piece of positive work of the type, What X says about
Y, there is an immediate possibility of specialization in both field and
subject. In field, because we are dealing with X, or a period of X's
life, or a movement in which X was involved, and so on. And in subject,
because it is the topic, Y, we are to study in X and not some other;
there will be divisions and their relationships and, before divisions,
something like an overall view; but a clear head, and monitoring by the
director, will enable the candidate to stay on the track. All that is
plain enough, but I would add that, from the viewpoint of this book, it
is important to determine not only field and subject but also the functional specialty to be pursued: is the work of the candidate to focus on
research, interpretation, history, or dialectic? Or on some conbination

---

11. Lonergan, Insight, pp. 173-74.

of some of these? This cannot always be determined in advance. It may
be that research has already been done, and the results made available
in critical texts, indices, bibliographies, and the like; but it may
turn out that it has not been done, and the candidate who wishes to
focus on, say, interpretation, will have a fair amount of research to do
just as a preliminary. In any case it is my experience that one is
greatly helped by Lonergan's categories in determining what exactly one
is doing.

Of course, one must keep an eye on local politics, if I may use
that word without pejorative connotations. There will perhaps be faculties in which research, as Lonergan defines it, would not be considered
a theological activity: Tischendorff's critical edition of the New
Testament would not then be admitted as a work of theology. There may
be other faculties in which it would be admitted under the umbrella of
theology, but not as proper material for a dissertation; the candidate
would be required, say, to enter into critical dialogue with the author
one has studied. "Criticism" is a rather highly operative word in many
academic circles; then, assembly of data counts for little, understanding is not perhaps a well-understood term, judgment as a reasonable
affirmation is not held in very high esteem, but a critical stance in
the dialectical sense is bound to be appreciated. I detect a critical
stance of my own in that sentence, and it is true that I believe we
regularly underestimate the worth of straightforward research, interpretation, and history. My "political" advice to candidates who would
regard dialectic as too ambitious now is therefore this. Let there be a
solid core of work in interpretation or history which will justify the
years of study in the personal formation it represents, which will
provide a strip of ground where candidates can take a stand, to assert
and defend what they know, which will also open up a career for future
dialectic and personal theology. Then, if the local situation demands
it, let them add a critical chapter, done of course as best as they can
do it but regarded nevertheless as a concession and not as the basis for
the "commencement" of a career.

Like a good dissertation writer, I too should stick to my topic,
which is the two ways of human development, and their structural articu-
lation in education. This chapter studied the topic in university life,
and this section studied it in a doctoral dissertation. I consider this
rather as the last exercise in formal education than as the inaugural

act of an academic career.   And   therefore I have argued for retaining
the way of tradition here,   to   the   extent   at least that the candidate
study an author whose   work   is   part   of   our   heritage.   This does not
exclude, indeed it   requires,   a   personal   contribution of the highest
caliber.   I would insist strongly on that: research, interpretation, and
history are not routine operations that can be passively performed by an
educated robot, they involve the   candidate   and require the exercise in
the most authentic style of   his or her attention, intelligence, reasonableness, and responsibility.   But   the   involvement is primarily in the
formal aspect; it regards the procedures   of   academic work.   It is only
the material on which these   functions   are   exercised that is not one's
own achievement but part of one's heritage.

4. "Life Is Real, Life Is Earnest"

       To consider the doctoral dissertation as the end of formal educa-
tion is not to deny that it is   also the "commencement" of a career.   To
what extent it really launches a young   man   or woman into a career is a
question that occupies the   university   world   more than a little: "doctor," after all, means one who teaches,   and there is a rather long step
from writing a dissertation to   teaching   a class of the new generation.
The professions have their specific form of this problem, and attempt to
solve it by the introduction   of   field education into the more academic
side; to what extent this is   desirable,   and   by what methods it can be
made most successful, are   questions   also   that occupy the educators in
that field.   Confronting a similar question on another battlefield altogether are those   engaged   in   the   now   well-established work of adult
education.

       Common to all three problem areas is a concern that the life of a
human being be not divided too sharply into a period of formal education
and a period in which one can say,   "Well, that's over; now I can get to
work" (or, in less responsible manner,   "Now   I   can have some fun").   A
book such as this   could,   therefore,   very   well   add a chapter at this
point on the relation of school to career, on the transition from one to
the other, on their lifelong   relationship,   etc.   But the chapter could
also be omitted;   the   decision   depends,   I   suppose,   on how weary the
author is or how weary he   suspects   his   readers to be.   My decision at

the moment is simply to write a short note on two aspects of life beyond
the schools. One is the business of law, the other the business of
Parliament. The first is suggested by my initial use of the lawcourt to
illustrate the structure of human consciousness, the other by my reference, recurring here and there, to the function of school in forming
citizens. But my private reason for the choice is the clarity with
which they provide a foil for showing the structure of experience,
understanding, reflection, and values in "real" life.

    I have indicated already my strictures, from a philosophical
point of view, on the procedures of the lawcourt. The role of the
opposing attorneys may be described as that of debaters carried into
real life, where the stakes are as real as they could possibly be,
involving the property, good name, freedom, perhaps the life itself of
the person on trial. But, though the stakes are so real and earnest,
the objective of each "debater" remains formally what it was in high
school, not the truth, but the winning presentation of a case for one
side. I repeat my high regard for the personal integrity of those I
know in the legal profession, and I repeat my recognition of the public
hope that by and large justice will be served by the adversarial system,
where "by and large" means that not too many guilty people are acquitted
and, above all, not too many innocent people are found guilty. I ask
only whether there may not be a better system, one that is more adapted
to the structured exigencies of human consciousness. My question, I am
happy to discover, has been anticipated in the legal profession itself:
quite by chance I stumbled on an article recently which informs me that
some countries are experimenting with the abandonment of the adversarial
system in favor of the collaborative pursuit of the truth itself, somewhat after the manner of scientific investigation.[12]   May the experiments succeed.

    I wish I could say something as lenient and hopeful about my
other example. It is our Parliamentary system on which we so prided
ourselves, a system whose workings are presented to us daily now in a
spectacle so pitiful and childish that one would be ashamed to observe
it in the kindergartens of our nation. A typical exchange during
question period might be the following. An honorable member: "Madam
Speaker, last week fifty-seven businesses went bankrupt in the nation;

---

12. I have lost, I regret to say, the reference to this article.

will the Minister of Business Affairs tell this House when his Government is going to abandon its blind, uncaring, irresponsible policy and
show some concern for the distress of our people?" To which the Minister might reply: "The honorable member cares nothing about the fifty-
seven businesses he mentions; but, as everyone knows, there is a by-
election tomorrow in the riding adjacent to his, and he is merely making
political capital to assist his friend in that election."

       I assure the reader that this is a mild and colorless exchange
compared to much that we hear in Parliament. Of course, the question
period is made to order for exhibiting oneself to one's constituents in
a neat package on television; of course, it is made to order also for
the media, which retail these neat one-minute packages the same evening
for the nation to admire. But things are not much better in the more
formal debates—the word, debate, is still used, incidentally, and
accurately used, for in most cases we see again a high school procedure
carried into real life, where again the stakes are high, and again truth
is not the objective of either side, but can only be a hope one reposes
in the system.[13]

       Can the system be improved or exchanged for a better? Are any
experiments being conducted that would be a counterpart to those I mentioned in the legal world? It does happen, in times of national crisis,
that a Union Government is formed, as if to say, "Our very survival is
at stake, and it's time to start acting like adults." One can imagine,
in a small-scale variation of this, two members, one from each opposing
party, stating their intention of joining together, on every significant
question, for an attentive, intelligent, reasonable, and responsible
study and, possibly, a joint stand.   One can dream of their attracting
other like-minded members from each party and becoming a force in Parliament. Is it just a dream? Would the party system, with its real
stabilizing influence in the nation, be threatened by such independence?
Would the "independents" be forced into, or gravitate toward, just
another party? Would their constituents back home, party stalwarts most
of them, accept such an independent exercise of attention, intelligence,

---

13. Need I say there are legitimate uses of the word, debate, even in
    real life? What I oppose is the transfer of the exercise from
    schoolroom practise to real-life situations without adding the
    component that orients the debater to reality, namely, the objective
    of truth.

reasonableness, and responsibility?[14]   I do not know the answer to
these and other questions that arise, but I would not abandon the hope
just because it is named a dream.   With Arthur O'Shaughnessy I would be
willing to say:

> We are the music-makers,
>   And we are the dreamers of dreams,

and to hope with him

> Yet we are the movers and shakers
>   Of the world for ever, it seems.

---

14. One should acknowledge, of course, the attentive, intelligent,
    reasonable, and responsible work done in Parliamentary committees;
    can the same attitude not be brought into the House of Commons, and
    even maintained before the television cameras?

CHAPTER SIX

THE CHRISTIAN DIMENSION

I have been talking of education pretty much as if it were a secular matter, with examples mostly from the prose and poetry taught in the public schools of the land and with emphasis, when there was question of tradition, on the tradition of the nation, the people, the local community, the family. But as grace perfects nature throughout all its ramifications, so the Christian word must follow education into every area and along its whole path from kindergarten to doctoral dissertation. All I have said is therefore to be given a Christian dimension, and I hope that all I have said is open to such a transposition. But there is no need for five separate chapters in which secular education receives, as it were, a Christian baptism; I need only sketch the added dimension that Christianity gives, and one chapter will do for that.

The specific viewpoint will remain that of the two ways of human development, which are, in fact, especially relevant to Christian education, or to any education that believes in a revelation given by God and has a history into which God has entered personally. But it will be convenient to change the order followed previously, beginning now with development from above on the basis of love and trust leading to beliefs and some measure of understanding. This is normal once the structure of consciousness is sufficiently established, and is almost mandatory in a study of Christian education where the differentiating factor, divine revelation, is pure gift to the human race, and not a human gift, in the sense of a tradition of civilization and culture from one generation to the next. Our order, then, will be education as heritage and education as achievement, and this in each of two stages: first, in procedures up to the end of secondary education, and then in what may be more properly called theological education.

133

1. Early Christian Education

The point with which I would begin is obvious, simple to understand, not hard to implement in practise, but much neglected, it seems,
in Catholic education of the past.   It is this, that the process from
above begins in love and trust.   We have seen how the child's love and
trust for its parents leads it to the rudimentary values and views that
guide its early conduct.   This applies also to the child's religious
attitudes, which, even more than other attitudes, depend on tradition
from the parents. But parental influence is not of itself an adequate
basis for the child's religious trust, faith, beliefs, and practise.
Only God, through the interior gift of the Spirit of Love, is such a
basis.[1]   So Christian education is the outer counterpart of this inner
gift, and must convey a sense of God as a loving God, one to whom the
child can relate in reciprocal love;   only in this way can the educator
lay a solid foundation for those Christian truths that will orient the
student, not only through school and university, but throughout life.

Catechetical authorities agree that much religious education in
the past, both in form and in content, would get low marks under this
heading. As to content, the simple index is the preaching that went
with earlier catechetics: one recalls those parish "missions" in which
the four last things, and especially death, judgment, and hell, were the
staple topic; the orientation of the whole mission to confession, maybe
to a general confession, did little to improve the situation. Many of
us have spent a good part of later life achieving a better perspective
on God, Christ, church, and sacraments.   As to form, that seems to have
been as inadequate as content.   Probably no one ever did hold that the
question-and-answer style of catechism had much to do with an attitude
of loving trust: it was simply a matter of a lesson to learn, a dull
lesson on such unintelligible topics as habitual and actual grace, but a
necessary one for the foundation, essentially doctrinal, of Christian

1. On the inner and the outer word of revelation see Lonergan, Method,
   pp. 112-115; the Christian understanding of what is there set forth
   in general religious terms, is given in the doctrine of Spirit and
   Son.

life. No doubt the better catechists quickened the dead word through stories of Jesus or of God's activity in Old and New Testaments. No doubt prophetic theologians, too, saw the need. Back in the 1600s one of them wrote a theologia mentis et cordis, a theology of mind and heart. Contenson, like his master, was a Dominican, and his textbook was the Summa theologiae of Thomas Aquinas. But his way of handling the text, after setting forth the doctrinal article (theologia mentis), was to add a series of pious reflections and applications that would appeal to the heart (theologia cordis).[2]   That is exactly the sort of thing the pastoral catechist tried, very laudably, to do. But my point remains and is reinforced by both catechist and theologian: each is struggling to correct a defect in the instrument used, to add a needed dimension not supplied with the tools at hand.

Few have a higher admiration than I for what Thomas Aquinas did in the thirteenth century. As for subsequent catechetical efforts, the church gratefully recalls and rightly praises the insistence of my own Ignatius Loyola on teaching children the doctrines of the faith. We remember too the the catechism of Peter Canisius in Catholic Reformation times. People do what they can in the situation they inherit, and not even saints can entirely escape the limitations their times impose. But need we live forever in the thirteenth or sixteenth century? At any rate there has sprung up in recent theology the topic of narrative, which is made to order for what modern catechists are striving to achieve: if you would convey an idea of a loving God, you must tell stories about God. What could be more simple? No one with any sense would try to make a child a patriot through a catechism of questions and answers about the nation, its history and constitution, its civic rights and duties. What do we do, as if spontaneously? We tell stories of heroes and heroines, of noble deeds, of great sacrifices, of a people's response to stirring speeches—and this in the justified confidence that love of country and loyalty to its cause will follow, creating a natural demand for more information. It is a mystery why this simple and obvi-

---

2. C. Lozier, "Contenson, Guillaume Vincent de," New Catholic Encyclopedia (New York: McGraw-Hill, 1967), 4:264.

ous method did not catch on more extensively in earlier catechism.[3]

Nevertheless, love and loyalty are not enough, either in civil or in religious society; we need also the truths we live by, and we need to receive them in tradition. This need applies to the highest culture and, no less, to the everyday business even of civil society, if each generation is not to begin all over again from the most primitive level of the human race. But it applies with absolute rigor to any religion which receives in revelation from God truths whose discovery is not a human achievement but a divine gift. I assume then as part of my Christian belief that God spoke, that something was said in the speaking, that what was said was, at least sometimes, a truth that would otherwise be hidden from our eyes. I have never understood the strange position that God is allowed to act, but not allowed to speak; that, if the right to speak be granted, still the Almighty is not allowed to say anything; that, if anything is said, it must be by way of rebuke or exhortation or the like, but must on no account be a proposition. And I find it little short of ludicrous that proposition after proposition should be uttered denying God the privilege of uttering propositions.

Having said that, maybe with more acerbity than was necessary, I wish to repudiate with equal vigor the opposite position of the fundamentalist, that revelation is a set of truths dictated from heaven to a diligently writing scribe. The description that appeals to me of the process of revelation is that it begins with God's gift of the Spirit of Love (resulting in what is aptly called an "inner" word of love in our hearts), that faith is the eye of this love (by analogy with Pascal's view that the heart has reasons that reason does not know), that, guided by this inner word certain privileged persons give expression to what God is doing among us (and thus there comes into being the "outer" word, what we commonly call the word of God), that the word of God becomes crystallized, often with labor over long periods, in the beliefs and creed of the people of God (a process that continues in the dogmas of

---

3. For a recent study of narrative theology see John Navone and Thomas Cooper, Tellers of the Word (New York: Le Jacq Publishing Inc., 1981). The secular catechism of a nation, which I regarded as so unlikely, actually occurred--so I am told, though I have forgotten by whom--in France after the revolution of 1789.

the church).[4] Naturally one's view of the way revelation works, of the
function of the anonymous inner word, of the images and narratives of a
tradition, of the creed of a people, and likewise of the role of
prophet, Messiah, evangelist, sacred writer, and church—what one's view
on all this is, will very considerably affect one's view on what Christian education should be and what procedures it should follow.[5]

      I would like to offer here a suggestion which will not be super-
fluous in a time of extremism, either that of radical opponents of dogma
or that of hardline reactionaries.   It amounts to an effort to combine
the best of new methods with something of the solid doctrinal core of
the old. Suppose then that we are teaching a young class who Jesus is,
and that we take as the basis of our lesson the story of the vineyard
owner who, having sent servant after servant to collect the rents, only
to have them beaten or even killed, says at last, "I will send my son;
they will respect my son."   And suppose the teacher, after whatever
explanation of the story is necessary to apply it to Jesus himself, were
to ask the class, "What would you say the difference was between Jesus
and the Old Testament prophets?   How would you put it in a plain and
simple statement?" Suppose the class takes its time on the topic (after
all, it is worth a fair amount of schooltime, maybe even a lifetime),
thinks as best it can, finds at length a statement to express its
belief. Suppose that then the teacher introduces them to some of Paul's
phrases, for example, that Jesus is God's own Son (even explaining
idios, the Greek for own), and invites comparison with what the pupils
have worked out.   Later still and after much pondering (considerably
later, therefore, for why hurry?), one might turn to John's term, God's
only or only-begotten Son, again inviting comparison with the pupils'
work. One might even go on to to Athanasius and his great principle, "The

---

4. This view is based very largely on positions set forth by Lonergan in
   Method, especially in chapter 4, "Religion."   There is a helpful
   account of the anonymity of the Spirit, and the need of the outer
   word, in "The Response of the Jesuit," A Second Collection, pp. 174-
   175.

5. I may note, in line with my general preference for "both ... and"
   rather than "either ... or," that to oppose narrative and dogma in
   such a way as to exclude one or the other is to impoverish oneself
   quite unnecessarily in things religious.

same things are said of the Son as are said of the Father." One would
surely be in a better position then to speak of the Nicene "consub-
stantial," supposing one thought it appropriate to speak of it at all at
this stage of education. The children's own efforts to derive a faith-
statement from a story would have been respected, but would also have
been slowly corrected to the point where they could "learn an answer"
from the catechism and appreciate the effort that went into its
phrasing, and indeed something of its meaning too.[6]

     The effort to say who Christ is could be expanded, with the
developing young pupil, into a more systematic effort to construct a
personal creed. We have plenty of models for this. The last two
decades have seen a spate of creeds, offered now by this person, now by
that, now by one group, now by another. All of them have the same purpose, to state for our times, in terms that show what God's work means
to us, what our ancestors first put into their various creeds centuries
ago. Thus, we have a creed from a labor school in India, which joyfully
affirms the wealth of God's world in a nation of great poverty, which
affirms life where infant mortality is high, which affirms one human
family though those professing this faith may be treated as second-class
citizens in other parts of the world.[7] So too we have "An African
Creed."[8] What is to prevent our own pupils from trying at the proper
time to draft their creed for their situation, and then bringing it into
comparison with the ancient creeds of the church as well as with other
modern efforts that might correct their mistakes and supply their
omissions?

     Already we are moving from below upward; it is time to attend
more consciously to that movement. This upward path cannot, in the
nature of the case, assume the importance in religious knowledge that it
has in secular, but that is no excuse for neglecting it. The aim, as

---

6. Lonergan has steadily regarded the Athanasian principle as a mile-
   stone in the development of doctrine; see, for example, "The Origins
   of Christian Realism," A Second Collection, pp. 250-251.

7. See The Expository Times 83 (1971-1972) 377.

8. U.S. Catholic, June, 1981, p. 31 (reprinted there from Vincent
   Donovan, Christianity Rediscovered).

nearly always, is to avoid extremes, represented historically by an
emphasis on dogma that suppressed experience and theology, or by a disregard of dogma in favor of one of that pair.   There is religious
experience: every moment is grace-filled, every action a response to or
a turning from grace, and the movements of grace enter consciousness;
but the experience of grace is not safely interpreted except with the
help of doctrines received from above.   And there is theological understanding; but understanding in the area of mystery can be only imperfect
and analogous.[9]

What the teacher can do is alert the young pupils to the grace-
aspect of their daily experience.   I cannot myself remember ever being
told of that aspect before I began formal study of theology. There may
have been a semblance of sound reason for the morbid fear in the church,
since the condemnation of modernism, of any appeal to experience. But
need we any longer be so skittish?   May we not hope that from now on it
will be part of religious education to help pupils observe in themselves
the workings of God's grace? Again, the teacher can alert pupils to the
need and role and limits of analogical understanding. Since the days of
the Lord Jesus himself, doctrines from above have always been explained
and must be explained by means of analogies, which offer the only understanding available of divine truth. But pupils can be taught the use of
analogies, can be taught too to criticize current analogies and helped
to form others, possibly not as good, but at least their own. I recall
with chagrin some of the analogies and images I have used in teaching
catechism; I think repentantly of the heresies that would follow if one
took them for doctrines; if I were teaching catechism again, one of my
ploys would be to engage the class in criticism of such faulty analogies—from which, after many examples, one could go on to teach more
effectively the role of analogy in general.

These brief reflections on the religious education of the young,
prior to studies that are formally theological, have had but one purpose: to set religious education in the same two-way framework as
secular education, with one movement that has its power and momentum

---

9. The position of the first   Vatican council, in its dogmatic constitution, Dei Filius (Cap. 4, De fide et ratione) has become classic;
   see Denzinger-Schönmetzer, Enchiridion symbolorum, no. 3016 (no. 1796
   in the Denzinger-Bannwart editions).

from what is given, in this case what is given by God and handed on by
the community of God's people; with another corresponding movement that
has its drive from a dynamism built into human nature, a dynamism that
will be frustrated if not allowed to achieve creatively its own potential; and with the two movements meeting and adjusting to one another in
mutual complementarity.

From above, then, there is a twofold gift: first the exterior
example and instruction of those we love and trust—parents, pastors,
prophets, Jesus the Lord; and secondly the interior presence of God's
love flooding our hearts through the gift of the Holy Spirit. Under
this double influence we come to personal adherence to God, to the Son
of God, to the church which is the Son's body. There is not only
adherence in loyalty; there is also acceptance of given truth, and there
is sustained effort to understand that truth. Now this effort to understand is the most personal and creative element in our struggle for
achievement, and in that sense the most significant component in the
movement from below. It is significant also in another important sense:
in the measure in which it succeeds we can construct for ourselves in
our time the truths we need to live by.

That latter aspect deserves far more attention than can be given
it here. Construction of religious truth is not an achievement of the
type found in science. It is rather the equivalent of Pope John's
objective as he set it forth for the bishops at the second Vatican
council: the changing expression of an unchanging deposit of faith.
Again, it is the equivalent of Bernard Lonergan's transposition of dogma
from the thought-patterns of another culture into those of our own.
And, yet again, it is related to the very traditional advice of catechists that we are to make our own the truths of our faith, or to the
exhortation of generations of retreat-masters that we should try to
realize our sinfulness, God's mercy, and so on—which itself is akin to
Newman's "real" apprehension of and assent to truth, as opposed to a
merely "notional" apprehension and assent.

The meeting of the two ways, their mutual adjustment, their har-
monious union, is a difficult and delicate task—itself part of our
achievement, but part also of the flow of good gifts that come down from
the Father of lights above. It appears in the individual believer
during the transition, if that occurs (for it is by no means a universal
achievement), from passive reception to creative personal possession.

It appears in a far more painful form in the wider church, when we go
through such a period of transition as the present, with aggiornamento
adopted as the motto for one side, and loyalty to a faith that was given
once and for all as the motto for the other. But difficulty and deli-
cacy are matters to challenge us, not excuses to opt out.

I suppose the area in which conflict arises most sharply, and its
resolution seems most imperative, is that of practise. Even before the
days of aggiornamento it was a delicate task to assist the young pupil
to move out of the pattern of monthly confession with the whole class at
school and into a more personal decision on frequenting the sacraments;
and now, what was once an occasional decision on this or that practise
has become a daily concern in many branches of conduct. Yet I suspect
that the area of ultimate battle will not be that of moral practises but
that of religious experience. God sent the Son visibly and the Spirit
invisibly; but they were both sent, and they both came into our world to
be really present there. Christians, naturally enough, have attended
more to the outer word linked with the Son than to the inner word linked
with the Spirit. We have to correct that imbalance.[10] We have also to
devote our creativity to the emergence, through song and dance, through
greeting and sharing, through outer signs of our inner bonding, to the
emergence through a thousand means of the outer concomitants of inner
religious experience. Dogmatic truth on the Spirit requires this of us,
while the example of the charismatics shows us, sometimes by excesses
but much more often by positive advances, the way we might go.

2. Theological Education

Let us turn (more directly anyway, for the topic has been creeping into our first section) to theological education, the religious
counterpart of the university education discussed in chapter five.
Here, if we continue the application of Bernard Lonergan's ideas, we may
seem to have our task already done for us in the eight functional

---

10. See my article, "Son and Spirit: Tension in the Divine Missions?"
    Science et Esprit 35 (1983), pp. 153-169, also published in Lonergan
    Workshop 5, edited by Fred Lawrence (Chico, CA: Scholars Press,
    1985), pp. 1-21.

specialties of his methodical theology.   Those specialties, after all,
not only relate one by one to the four levels of human consciousness,
but are so divided into two basic phases that the four specialties of
the first phase regard what we receive from the past and the other four
constitute our effort to speak to our own times—have we not in this
division the downward and upward movements that structure the whole of
this present study?

> If one is to harken to the word, one must also bear witness to
> it. If one engages in lectio divina, there come to mind quaes-
> tiones.   If one assimilates tradition, one learns that one
> should pass it on. If one encounters the past, one also has to
> take one's stand toward the future.   In brief, there is a
> theology in oratione obliqua that tells what Paul and John,
> Augustine and Aquinas, and anyone else had to say about God and
> the economy of salvation.   But there is also a theology in
> oratione recta in which the theologian, enlightened by the past,
> confronts the problems of his own day.[11]

Yes, here indeed we have the two movements of tradition and innovation,
but theological education raises a further question, and besides,
division of the work into the phases of mediating and mediated theology
(as Lonergan calls them) presents a puzzle that we have not yet sufficiently considered. Preliminary notes to clarify these two points will
help clear the decks for the discussion of this section.

The first note regards the specialties as a whole and the place
of the eighth in that unity.   The book, Method, was written to aid the
creative doing of theology.   But doing theology creatively, and teaching
theology to students, even teaching it creatively, are not the same
thing, however much they need one another and however much the theologian may benefit from combining the two.   Teaching theology is largely a
communication of theology already done, even when students are encouraged to go further on their own; and, since communications is one of the
eight specialties, teaching theology is part of doing it, but only as
one function out of eight.   The reverse, however, does not hold: all
teaching of theology is doing it, but not all doing theology is teaching
it—at least not in the present sense of university teaching, though no
theologian is such a recluse as not to try to communicate with his or
her peers. Thus, the famous Dictionnaire de théologie catholique was an

---

11. Lonergan, Method, p. 133.

effort at doing, and at communicating, theology of a certain type; but
even in an updated form it could hardly form the core of a theological
education aimed at a baccalaureate.   We cannot, therefore, assume that
Lonergan's eightfold division of theological tasks has done all the work
envisaged in this section of the present study.

        The second note regards the two phases and their supposed corre-
spondence with the upward and downward movements of human development.
For there is a puzzle here: the passage above, which I quoted to show
Lonergan's rationale for the two phases, seems to show exactly the
opposite of what we intend. That is, the four specialties of the first
phase, research, interpretation, history, and dialectic, should move
upward with the dynamism of consciousness, from experience (research to
establish data) through interpretation and history to dialectic. But
Lonergan explains this first phase as a whole to make it a matter of
receiving from the past: we harken to the word, engage in reading,
assimilate tradition, and encounter the past.   Similarly, the four
specialties of the second phase, foundations, doctrines, systematics,
and communications, should all move downward in the opposite direction.
But again Lonergan explains the second phase as a whole to make it a
matter of achievement rather than of receiving: we are to confront the
problems of our own day and take our own stand toward the future.

        This by no means trivial puzzle forces us to conceive more
clearly a distinction that has hovered in the background of our study,
became explicit in our remarks on the doctoral dissertation, but has not
yet been brought sufficiently into focus—the distinction, namely,
between the operations of the theological specialties and the materials
on which they operate.   The operations are always those of the four
levels of consciousness and, insofar as research, interpretation, history, and dialectic follow the order of the four levels, their movement
is from below upward: similarly, insofar as foundations, doctrines,
systematics, and communications proceed from the level of values to that
of experience, their movement is from above downward. But the materials
on which we operate in the first phase of theology are largely the
legacy of the past; as believers, and merely passive believers, we may
receive them without research, leave their interpretation to church
authorities, take for granted the tradition that delivers them to us,
and accept without challenge the beliefs and way of life they decree for

us. Then there is little difference between first phase and second, but
then also we are avoiding the work of theology.

Now to call it the work of theology is to say that we aim at a
certain achievement. And, in fact, theologians had to work strenuously
to achieve, say, a critical text of the New Testament; they still work
to interpret it, to trace the tradition from our beginnings to the
present, to analyze the horizons of the successive interpreters, and
thus to present to our time a purified and transposed message, as the
achievement of the theological enterprise. But that statement includes
the second phase of theology as part of the achievement. True, it is in
virtue of God's love here and now flooding their hearts, and of the
present gift of faith which is their eye of love, that theologians
accept the message of tradition as their own, affirm it for their times,
insert it into the context of contemporary culture, and preach it to the
men and women of their day. This latter course is truly a movement
downward from the level of values to that of "experience made mature and
perceptive." Still, it is work, and the transposed and newly presented
message is a theological construction, the achievement of men and women.
The puzzle of Lonergan's mediating and mediated phases has therefore
issued in an important clarification: all theology is work toward an
achievement, but in the first phase a natural drive toward truth and
value guides our operations, while in the second the indwelling Spirit
takes the lead.

One more preliminary note: while a philosophy of education may be
more enduring, and tactics at the other pole vary greatly, a strategy of
education, which is our concern, has to be somewhat adaptable while
remaining under the guidance of the enduring philosophy. We will continue, then, to base our strategy on the complementary movements of
developing human consciousness; but we must attend also to the special
needs of a time that is especially crucial for theology. The discipline
that to secular eyes is so monolithic and unchanging has entered upon a
transition hardly paralleled since the Palestinian apostles went out to
preach the word to the Hellenic world, or since the logic and metaphysics of Aristotle invaded patristic theology in the early middle
ages. Further, while there are those who hope that the crisis is
passing and that theology will soon settle down, my own view is that the
transition has just begun, that it will continue, that it ought to continue, that what our times call for is a total reconstruction of

theology, even that of the first phase.   True, the achievements in
research have been enormous, interpretation in many cases has attained a
near consensus, and history is done quite respectably.   But all three
have to be rethought as functions of a total process; they have to be
related to one another and to an ensuing dialectic; above all, they have
to be integrated with a new mediated theology.   But dialectic is only
now struggling out of anonymity toward its own identity and, until it
achieves that identity and can go about its proper work in freedom, we
cannot lay foundations for the transposed doctrines we need, and so the
whole second phase of mediated theology remains in embryo.[12]   There is
irony in the fact that, while modern theology is much better equipped to
handle the past than it was two centuries ago, students today are little
interested in that phase of study: it is present experience that at-
tracts their interest, almost exclusively so.   The educator cannot
ignore this fact; at the university level we can no longer play the role
of wise and benevolent dictators, even supposing we are as wise and
benevolent as one could wish.   We can teach mature young men and women
only what they are willing to learn.   But I would insist that our task
then becomes that of teaching them to be more willing to learn about
their past.   If we are to assume the responsibility that belongs to us
as educators, we must take a stand for the value of the legacy, and for
its communication in theological education.

        So much for preliminaries; we may turn now to our main purpose.
It concerns strategy rather than tactics, the deployment of basic human
operations rather than curricula and pedagogical techniques.   That
applies with special force in the fluid field of theological studies,
and at a level on which studies divide into many fields and subjects,

---

12. Meanwhile, of course, we remain Christians and adherents of our
    church tradition, rejoicing in the gift of God's love which we
    receive quite independently of theological achievements.   We
    likewise continue to treasure the accumulation of documents we
    receive from the past; it is indeed these that we are best equipped
    to handle in theology, through our well-established procedures of
    research, interpretation, and history.   We are not so well equipped
    to handle the present; not only does the dialectic that would orient
    us still lack tested procedures, but also the battle to give a
    proper role to the Holy Spirit and present experience, while going
    favorably, has not yet ended in full victory.

with multiplying options. Most of what I have to say, then, will follow
the four levels of consciousness. That does not mean that the corresponding specialties are to be taught in chronological sequence, or even
kept separate from one another in distinct courses. It means only that
they represent distinct activities which must affect our understanding
of theological education.   It is probably true, however, that their
distinction will not be made clear to the student without distinct
treatment in one course or another.   We begin, therefore, with the upward movement which will consist in a personal appropriation, through
research, interpretation, history, and dialectic, of the theological
tradition. We leave to second place that input from the Spirit and
present experience which is needed for the downward movement of mediated
theology.

       First, then, in order of consideration but not of pedagogy, comes
assembly of the data, where the data are not the experience of daily
life (of those, later in the chapter) but the documents of tradition.
Here one has to insist (while regretting the need to insist) on intimate
familiarity with the basic documents.   A typist cannot operate efficiently in ignorance of the keyboard; but, what the keyboard is to the
typist, that, more or less, the basic documents are to the theologian at
the research stage. The memory, then, must be drenched with the New
Testament, have easy access to the Old, be familiar with early creeds
and liturgies, with representative writings of the fathers, and with the
chief conciliar decrees.   It is impossible to perform reliably as a
general practitioner of theology, in ignorance of the differences
between Paul and James, of the way the creeds grew, of the emergence and
resolution of the great debates in the church.   One may add that it is
impossible too for the specialist to be other than a narrow-minded
specialist without such general knowledge.

       Nor can one plead impossibility, for I am not requiring an ency-
clopedic knowledge. There is a graduated scale of requirements. For
some of the tradition one can do no better than an overall view: such
might be the case for the post-Chalcedonian documents in Christology.
At the other end of the scale stands the New Testament, which should be
as familiar to the students as the streets of their own city. In
between lie other documents. There is need of good judgment, but facul-
ty advisors are there to supply that.   There is need most of all of
personal work and basic reading in the student's leisure hours, and I

stress the word, basic. Again, I regret having to insist on something
so fundamental. The insistence ought to be superfluous, but is not: I
have seen too many students talking fluently about the latest articles
in theology (articles, be it noted, that will not be the latest ten
years from now) but unable to find 2 Peter in the New Testament, let
alone give any reliable judgment on the date of its composition.

Then there is interpretation, competence in which is a slow
growth and full mastery of which belongs to the specialist. Still, the
student can achieve a general sense of the thought-patterns peculiar to
particular times and cultures, and even to particular authors. A general sense that is real and not just notional will emerge, not from
memorizing points of difference, but from study of well-chosen represen-
tatives of biblical, patristic, medieval, and modern writers. A more
thorough study of the characteristics of one particular author ought to
be attempted. This would be a matter of reading and re-reading the
author--Paul, let us say--of turning to those who are Pauline scholars,
of turning back to oneself in the effort to identify one's own patterns
of thinking, of returning to Paul, and so advancing in a gradual process
of growth and correction to the point of identifying differences, of
realizing what an author is likely to say, and thus recognizing spurious
or quoted passages. I remember once reading the commentary of Aquinas
on 1 Corinthians, in an old edition which was all I could lay hands on,
and coming to paragraphs that were simply so strange, so unexpected,
that I said to myself, "This is not Thomas Aquinas." Indeed, it was
not; his commentary on three chapters of 1 Corinthians is lost, and the
editor had filled in the lacuna. He had acknowledged that in his
preface, but at that point I had not read the preface.

With such a sense of particular times and authors, and not without such a sense, we are able to do history. This is quite manageable
within the New Testament itself, but one must overcome the tendency to
regard the word of God as a timeless entity outside history, and one
must ruthlessly abandon the traditional order of the New Testament
writings. In regard to the latter, what the beginner needs is a collection of the twenty-seven books set in chronological order, so far as
that can be determined. One could have them inserted in a loose-leaf
binder for changing the order according to particular views on, say, the
letter of James, but there would be little difficulty about the rough
skeleton locating key writings. The psychic effect of transposing the

books from the conventional to the chronological order would be considerable, I think, for the student of historical evolution.

The chief difficulty in history, once we leave the New Testament,
is the sheer quantity of the materials.   The teacher will have to
select, the selection must be strategic, and that requires a more than
ordinary mastery of the whole field.   It is easy to assign for study,
let us say, the occurrence of the terms, law and grace, in 1 Thessa-
lonians and Romans; the students will discover the startling difference
between the two letters and will themselves spontaneously ask, What
happened in between to account for the change? But what can one do with
the voluminous patristic writings?   The case, I suggest, is not hopeless. One could promote interest in history just by scanning the titles
in a patristic anthology, observing what topics emerged at particular
times, and asking why they did so.   Why, for example, did Basil, Didy-
mus, and Ambrose suddenly start writing on the Holy Spirit, when there
was no precedent for that in the titles of earlier works? The same
strategy might be employed for the even more voluminous writings of our
own times. With the aid of the indices now available, or even by running through the tables of contents of periodicals, the student might
become quite curious to learn why, forty years ago, there should suddenly be a spate of articles on kerygmatic theology, or why, twenty years
later, there should be another on the death of God—and equally why the
spate should dry up almost as suddenly as it began.

History is concerned mainly with change, but more generically
with what happened—which includes also recurrences and so evidence of
continuity. The teacher will promote a sense of this also in the
student, and a love for the unity across space and time of those through
whom the message is transmitted. Thus, one might select a fragment from
a letter of Ireneus to a certain Florinus, in which he recalled how they
had sat together at the feet of Polycarp, while the latter discoursed on
what he had learned from John and the others who had seen the Lord; it
is a moving paragraph on the continuity from the Lord through the apostles to Polycarp, and so, a century and a half after the resurrection,
to the aging Ireneus.[13]   A more doctrinal example: Athanasius explained

13. For convenient reference see M. J. Rouët de Journel, Enchiridion
    patristicum, (Barcelona: Herder, 1962), no. 264. Also, Migne's
    Patrologia graeca, 7, 1225.

to Serapion the principle that the relationship the Son has to the
Father is the same as that which the Spirit has toward the Son; now this
very principle is found repeated some years later in Basil's treatise on
the Holy Spirit.[14] It is desirable, of course, that the students "discover" such continuity through their own efforts—for which purpose the
teacher must not only have a copious supply of instances, but know how
to lead the class to their "discovery."

What part should dialectic play in theological education? The
level is now that of conflicts and options, on the way to personal
decision, and one supposes that students have made their basic commitment years earlier. Still, commitments have to be renewed continually,
so the need for encounter and challenge is ongoing. In one sense the
need is met almost automatically: one can hardly read the New Testament
without encounter and challenge. So one is inexorably led to respond,
or left in a state of refusing to respond. But in another important
sense the need is not met without theological education. For every
witness in our tradition, including the Lord Jesus himself, spoke or
wrote within a horizon, and all that they said or wrote must be understood, judged, and evaluated within that horizon, if we are to transpose
it faithfully to our own. The believing student, with the believing
professor, and as the latter's disciple and partner, will conduct this
dialectic in a spirit of critical reverence. To be critical, merely to
be critical, in order to conform to academic priorities and demonstrate
one's openness, is the privilege of the unbeliever; to examine the documents dialectically, while regarding them as a precious heritage given
and received in love and trust, is the role of the believer.

This applies even to the ipsissima verba of Jesus, so far as they
may be recoverable through the careful work of exegetes and historians.
In fact, it is a distinct benefit of a dialectic properly applied in the
effort to determine the horizon of Jesus, that it will save his word
from mauling by the unbelieving critic. To understand, for example, the
horizon within which the Lord Jesus used the apocalyptic imagery of
stars falling from heaven will enable us to apprehend the truth he
intended and to transpose it into imagery more suited to our times. But
how is that horizon determined? Not without the New Testament accounts,

---

14. See again Rouët de Journel, Enchiridion, no. 783 for Athanasius and
    no. 951 for Basil. Or Migne, Patrologia graeca, 26, 625 and 32,
    148.

of course, but not without a theology that goes considerably beyond what exegesis and history can discover in the immediate data of the New Testament. We shall return to this question in a moment.

After the first phase of theology, the second; after the mediating theology of the tradition, the mediated theology that one makes one's own. How does one make it one's own? How does such personal involvement affect theological education? In particular, how does mediated theology relate to our basic upward and downward movements of human development?

This is the phase of input from the Holy Spirit, of inner religious experience, and of appropriation by the theologian of the converted interiority that is due to the presence of the Spirit. It is this input, along with the purified and assimilated tradition, that provides the foundation for the downward movement through doctrines, systematics, and communications. I have remarked on the irony that students, who could be taught to handle the mediating phase, are so eager now to plunge into personal theology.[15] Let me remark on the parallel irony that career theologians and professors, who are in a position to develop a second-phase theology that is not just subjectivist but truly mediated by the tradition, are so reluctant to launch into the deep with the Holy Spirit, but cling cautiously to "solid" doctrine, the "tried and true" formulas in the legacy of our ancestors. But, if theology mediates between religion and culture,[16] if it is a bridge from one shore to another, then, be it ever so solidly built, it will not span the river if the original target on the opposite side has moved downstream in the intervening centuries.

Now in this never-ending work of adaptation that is obedience to the Spirit, one will have to avoid mere subjectivism. For the reactionary Catholic this is easy: one obeys the Spirit by obeying the magisterium of the church. Those less reactionary will realize that the

---

15. Such generalizations are hardly uttered before they are out-of-date; trends change with succeeding generations of students, and generations in this field follow one another every five years or less.

16. Thus, the first line of Lonergan's Method, p. xi: "A theology mediates between a cultural matrix and the significance and role of a religion in that matrix."

whole church is involved in adaptation, and ask how the church avoids
subjectivism. The answer may then be given in the broad terms of a
teaching competence and authority. This authority, again, may be understood more as a fixed possession (the Thomist virtus: analogous to the
skill of the ball carrier in football), or more as a capacity to respond
flexibly (the Thomist donum: analogous to running interference, adapting
one's movements to those of another); further, the authority may be
understood to belong to the people of God or to be located in those who
speak for the people. But one way or another, it is the Spirit who is
behind it all, who, no matter what the gifts or to whom they are given,
maintains a sovereign freedom which we must learn to trust. Why is that
so difficult? Is the Spirit not as really and truly sent as the Son, as
really and truly present in the world of creation?[17]

When we come, then, to the second phase of theology we are in the
business of spirituality. There is no use blinking that fact, not in
these times anyway when scores of theological schools have awakened to
their lack of and need for a program of spiritual formation, a formation
that is not a pietism extrinsic to academic content but a built-in element of theological education. It is a major attraction, I believe, of
Lonergan's theological method, that it can provide for this element.
Not that method replaces the divine initiative: "The apologist's task is
neither to produce in others nor to justify for them God's gift [of] his
love. Only God can give that gift, and the gift itself is self-justifying." What applies to the apologist applies more widely to all theologians: "they do not bestow God's grace."[18] The method is designed,
not to replace God's gift, but to cooperate with it, and to do so in the
two ways (input on the objective side, input on the subjective side)
that correspond to the two divine missions: the visible mission of the
Son into the world of the objective, the invisible mission of the Spirit
into the world of the subjective.

---

17. A basic difficulty has been that we lacked a philosophy of interi-
    ority with which to construct a theology of the Spirit's presence
    within us, and thus became theological behaviorists in regard to the
    Spirit—I may refer again to my article, "Son and Spirit: Tension in
    the Divine Missions?" (note 10, above).

18. Lonergan, Method, p. 123.

The result one hopes for, from this combination, would be doctrines in the sense of Lonergan's sixth functional specialty, which are
not just the ancient dogmas and gospel truths, but are not different
truths either: "if anyone preaches a gospel at variance with the gospel
which [we have] received, let him be outcast!" (Gal 1:9). Theology is
the gospel truth transposed to our times and made personal truth through
being founded in the personal gift of the Spirit. Many will be concerned about the way this transposition is to be effected; may I suggest
some reliance here on the advice, solvitur ambulando? If we go forward
in at least tentative acceptance of the accumulated scholarship of
researchers, interpreters, and historians, in the submission of this
work to the crucible of dialectic, in the effort to relate it to the
present experience of the Spirit in the community of believers, we just
might find that questions of transposition, and of the authority to make
them and rule on them, have ceased to be as thorny as they seem in
advance. These reflections apply more directly to emerging theology
than to theological education, but that is inevitable in the present
chaos; what an educator can do is keep students alive to the process,
and endeavor with them to work out some sample transpositions of earlier
modes of expression.

Then there is systematics, that much battered specialty, one for
which the need, however, emerges more clearly than ever after our inun-
dation for two centuries by positive studies. A good example is the
question of the consciousness of Christ. It is quite useless for
positivists to decree the impossibility of saying anything intelligent
and rational on the mind of Christ; the efforts continue despite the
declarations of impossibility. But the very variety of conclusions from
those efforts does give a handle to the objectors: if explanations are
going to differ so widely, is not that itself a reason for declaring the
project vain, the mission impossible?

For one who thinks in Lonergan's categories, what is lacking is
the upper blade of heuristic method, the blade commonly supplied by
systematics—in this case, a theory of consciousness able to organize
the data on Christ in scripture and tradition. Personally, I do not
know of any major piece of thinking in modern times that is at once so
illuminating and so widely neglected as Lonergan's study of the con-

sciousness of Christ.[19] This book is not the place to debate personal
views on particular questions of theology but behind the personal view
lies a more public matter of principle: the need that thoughtful
believers experience for theological giants to guide them in system-
atics--they look up, like hungry sheep that are not fed, for the word of
reason to unite with their gospel faith.   Giants are hard to come by in
any field, especially giants of the stature of Thomas Aquinas. But
Aquinas himself was possible only as the peak of a mountain range, and
there are many mountains there to climb in the modern scene.   To return,
then, to our topic, I consider that educators betray their trust when
they offer the student only a smorgasbord of articles from various view-
points. Of course, there must be due recognition of theological pluralism, but that is about as helpful to the student as the advice to
listeners that I hear every Sunday on the radio: go to church today; go
to the church of your choice, but go to some church. If I offer similar
vague advice to educators, the educators themselves have to be more
helpful: they have to initiate their students into a theology that is
systematic and comprehensive, one that will enable them to see life
steadily and see it whole.

     Finally, there is communications: though theological education is
itself an exercise in this, educators are not thereby exempted from
speaking about it, just as any school of educational studies must talk
about education as well as practise it. Some points to bear in mind are
these. First, the objective of communications, as understood here, is
not simply to convey information but to build up a community of faith.
When we aim at the former, we sooner or later come upon the anomaly of a
Jewish boy required to study Christian doctrine, since he chose to
attend a Christian school, and at the year's end getting the prize in
that subject. But when the aim is right we understand that through
communication "there is constituted community and, conversely, community
constitutes and perfects itself through communication."[20] Another point

---

19. Most fully in Bernard Lonergan, De constitutione Christi ontologica
    et psychologica (Rome: Gregorian University Press, 1956); more
    briefly, but with some revisions, in his De Verbo incarnato (Rome:
    Gregorian University Press, 1964), Thesis 10a.

20. Lonergan, Method, p. 363.

is the pluralism of cultures and of differentiations of consciousness within a given culture. For the structure of consciousness is one thing, the vicissitudes of its development another: the structure is the invariant locus of an extremely variable history. There is, of course, an immediate need in the classroom itself to take account of the difference between professor and students. They may think in a commonsense mode, and he or she in a more theoretic way; or—a preferable situation—they may have begun to think theoretically, and he or she in the methodical way that allows one to relate common sense and theory.

We are verging now on classroom tactics and, while that is not my field, I think that something must be said, almost as a matter of justice, on such a practical question as that of curriculum. What remote advice, in terms of the larger strategy I have been discussing, can be given on this question? About all one can say is that there must be a prudential mix of overall courses and detailed studies. There has to be a fairly staple diet of overall courses, to avoid the stigma of knowing more and more about less and less; this applies to the field when there is question of materials (for example, the field of the Old Testament) and to the subject when there is division by conceptual classification (theology of the sacraments, and so on). But there must be room also for detailed studies, enough courses at least to show students how such studies are conducted and how little of scholarship is learned from overall surveys. I have given suggestions already for exercises in interpretation and history. I would add now a recommendation for distinct exercises in all six functional specialties from research, through interpretation and history, to dialectic, foundations, and doctrines. Nor should the educator feel overwhelmed: I am asking for only six units out of a presumed program of thirty for a baccalaureate in theology. As for systematics, some kind of system should structure all the doctrinal studies, but how much explicit attention this aspect will receive is so much determined by varying philosophical background that it seems rather useless to attempt any further precision here.

As the reader knows, such practical questions multiply without end, and there is no point in my following the multiplying throng; they must be left to the expertise of the professional educator. But it was important, for clarity on the strategy of education, to see how they relate to the main lines of the grand plan structured according to the basic and complementary movements of upwardly oriented achievement and downwardly oriented tradition.

APPENDIX

SCHOOL WITHOUT GRADUATES: THE IGNATIAN SPIRITUAL EXERCISES

Education can be conceived in a stricter sense as formal education, the instruction given to the young (most often) in an institutional setting, or it can be conceived in a wider sense to include the instruction one receives from life itself throughout one's years. The two modes should not be too sharply differentiated and, in fact, we are now learning (are being educated) to see them more as parts or aspects of a single process. Even the sharp distinction that once was operative between the teaching and the learning church has lost much of its relevance; we are too sadly aware that the whole church is a learning church. So it is no longer a matter of education versus real life: real life is education, and becoming educated is real living.

Then, of course, the question occurs, What is real life? And we cannot but recall the "definition" Jesus gave in his great prayer at the Last Supper: "This is eternal life: to know thee who alone art truly God, and Jesus Christ whom thou hast sent" (Jn 17:3). If life and education belong to one process, there should be an educative program not just for secular life and religious doctrine, but for eternal life as well. I hope that chapter six has already made this clear. In support of that chapter there is also the old tradition of calling a monastery a schola Christi, school of Christ. In any case a work that purports to give a transcendental and therefore universal strategy of education can hardly omit a study of this "higher learning" given in a school which offers no degrees, and graduates no one till it delivers its pupils into the life where knowledge is no longer partial, but "whole, like God's knowledge of me" (1 Cor 13:12). I recognize, however, that such a consideration does not lie in the field of immediate interests for some of my readers, so I include it in an appendix which they may more readily omit.

My practise here and there in the book was to take a paradigm
case and use it in illustration of the principles which are my main
concern: the paradigm in itself is then of quite secondary importance.
Such was the case, for example, in my copious references to the public
schools of sixty years ago in Ontario and New Brunswick. I propose to
use a paradigm again and, if it were to be only a paradigm, one possible
instance among many, it would again be of minor importance. But I may
be forgiven for regarding this case as a bit special, for it is the
Spiritual Exercises of St. Ignatius Loyola.[1]

The saints have given us many roads to follow in knowledge of God
and discipleship of Christ: the rule of St. Benedict, the way of St.
Francis of Assisi, and dozens of others down to our times and the
renewed, or perhaps wholly new, efforts to trace a spirituality of
priesthood, of secular institutes, of the laity, and so on. All of them
are needed, none of them claims to exhaust the potential of what God
offers us in the Son and their Spirit. But what gives the Spiritual
Exercises a more universal application in the school of Christ and a
study of education, is that they do not aim at making exercitants
Ignatian in the particular sense of making them Jesuits; the aim rather
is to help them find God's will. What is God's will in each case? It
is not to be determined in advance. Maybe it is to be a doctor, lawyer,
space traveler; maybe to enter politics, or to be a missionary nurse in
the Third World; maybe, among other possibilities, to follow Ignatius in
the order he founded. One does not tell the Holy Spirit the directions
one wishes to receive; one listens and learns. From this viewpoint the
Spiritual Exercises may serve as an especially useful paradigm.[2]

_____

1. The Latin title is Exercitia Spiritualia. There have been countless
   editions and translations. A recent and authoritative edition is
   found in Monumenta Historica Societatis Iesu, Vol. 100, (Rome:
   Institutum Historicum Societatis Iesu, 1969). This gives four of the
   most ancient texts (including the autograph) in parallel columns, and
   adds the paragraph numbers that have become standard. For the
   English quotations in this Appendix, I will use Louis J. Puhl, S.J.,
   The Spiritual Exercises of St. Ignatius: A New Translation,
   (Westminster, MD: The Newman Press, 1962), and will give the
   numbering of the 1969 Roman edition (which Puhl also was able to use
   in advance, p. viii).

2. While I speak of the Exercises as a paradigm for the educational processes of the Holy Spirit, I would point out that in themselves they
   are rather an organon, and one to which Lonergan's theological

What are these famous Exercises?   The term, spiritual exercise,
refers to all such activities as examination of one's conscience,
praying, preparing one's soul to find the divine will, and the like.[3]
So Ignatius tells us. But his own list comes nowhere near revealing the
secret of his little book; that surely lies in the psychological and
ascetical arrangement of the exercises—in the order both of the four
weeks and of the exercises within each week—and is most brilliantly
revealed in the key strategic exercises that give the whole set its
efficacy. The four weeks deal successively with sin and its consequences, with the public life of Christ, with his passion, with his
resurrection and ascension; they are enclosed by a kind of prologue
(Principle and Foundation) and a kind of epilogue (Contemplation to Gain
Love), though I do not mean "prologue" and "epilogue" to suggest that
they are dispensable.   Certain key exercises are regarded as Ignatian
specialties: those on the Kingdom of Christ (introducing the Second
Week), or on Two Standards (bringing the options of life to a focus),
and so on. The book also contains a great deal of ascetical advice,
rules for conduct in particular circumstances, and the like; but my
concern here is with the integral structure of the exercises and their
total dynamics.

This schematic presentation will hardly convey to the reader the
power of the Exercises or show sufficient reason for choosing them as
paradigm: here perhaps a little personal history will be more helpful.
During forty-seven years I have made the Exercises every year, regularly
for a period of eight days, twice for the full thirty days. One cannot
go over and over the same ground, reading the same directions, using the
same formulas, without pondering and pondering again the sense and
drift, the meaning and purpose, of the whole maneuver, and the secret of
its efficacy. I recall a remark of Newman's, simple and profound in
Newman's way, about the baptismal formula and its influence on Trini-

---

organon bears some resemblance: as the Exercises do not tell the
exercitant what to find as God's will but only how to find it, so
Lonergan's book does not tell theologians what to find but only how
they might find it. Not accidentally, both works are referred to as
methods.

3. Ignatius Loyola, Spiritual Exercises, no. 1.

tarian theology: "it was impossible to go on using words without an
insight into their meaning."[4]   That describes exactly my own experience
with the Exercises, so much so that I can best set forth my present
point as the most recent in three formal attempts to analyze them, to
gain "an insight into their meaning."

I first attempted a comprehensive analysis in my student days,
when I was reveling in the Prima secundae of St. Thomas. Aquinas himself constructed his psychology very much along the lines of the end/
means structure of Aristotelian thinking, greatly enriching Aristotle as
he did so and adding a wealth of psychology that we are far from having
exhausted. Naturally my first analysis followed this pattern, centering
on the "election" which is the heart of the Exercises and can be un-
packed and set forth according to the Thomist psychology Ignatius
learned at the University of Paris.   Thus the purpose of human life is
stated at the very beginning in the Principle and Foundation (and
repeated at the Election) in these terms: "Man is created to praise,
reverence, and serve God our Lord, and by this means to save his
soul."[5] The same opening paragraphs reduce everything else on earth to
the level of means to be chosen so far as they lead to the desired end.
With this orientation restored and made operative by divine grace, the
First Week enters into the end/means structure through a study of sin as
a turning away from the end, and of repentance as a turning back to it.
The Second Week functions more positively as a pursuit of the end; more
specifically, as a pursuit of the end through the means given us by God
in the only Son.   This corresponds closely to the structure of the
Thomist Summa theologiae: "first we will treat of God; secondly, of the
progress of rational creatures toward God; thirdly, of Christ who, insofar as he is man, is our way of tending toward God."[6] The great strategic exercises can be fitted well enough into this pattern: the options
presented by Christ in the two main life-styles, one in which he is

---

4. Tracts Theological and Ecclesiastical (London: Longmans, Green and
   Co., 1924), p. 152.

5. Spiritual Exercises, no. 23, and see no. 169.

6. Summa theologiae, I, q. 2, Prologus: "primo tractabimus de Deo;
   secundo, de motu rationalis creaturae in Deum; tertio, de Christo,
   qui, secundum quod homo, via est nobis tendendi in Deum."

obedient to his parents at home, and one in which he leaves them at the
age of twelve to be about his Father's work, can be seen as a deliberation about means, the Thomist consilium;[7] the Two Standards illuminate
the hidden processes at work in seemingly innocent means;[8] the Three
Pairs of Men are a persuasive exercise leading to decision.[9]

There is much to ponder in a Thomist approach to the Exercises,
nor do I think any of the positive Thomist input need be abandoned. But
it serves less effectively in explanation of the Third and Fourth Weeks,
which have to be seen in this analysis as mainly confirmatory of the
Election and an extension of that way which is the imitation of Christ;
indeed, it does not fully exploit the virtualities of even the First and
Second Weeks. This latter point occupied me again quite a few years
later, when Lonergan's Method had come out and I was reveling now in the
new ideas of Dialectic, his fourth functional specialty.[10] My new
analysis moved therefore from Thomist tools to those provided by Lonergan, from a process structured by ends and means to one structured by
dialectic, from the exercise of what is called horizontal liberty to
that of vertical: "Horizontal liberty is the exercise of liberty within
a determinate horizon and from the basis of a corresponding existential
stance. Vertical liberty is the exercise of liberty that selects that
stance and the corresponding horizon."[11] Thomist psychology does
provide for such a shift in horizon, describing it as the substitution
of one end for another, but this is not a major concern of the Prima
secundae. It is a major concern of Method, where the shift from one
horizon to another is an about-turn in the life of theologians and
determinative of their mediated theology; it is not just genetic, a

---

7. Spiritual Exercises, no. 134; the Thomist consilium: Summa theologiae, I-II, q. 14.

8. Spiritual Exercises, no. 136.

9. Spiritual Exercises, no. 149.

10. I published this effort under the title, "Dialectic and the Ignatian
    Spiritual Exercises," Science et Esprit 30 (1978) 111-127; also in
    Lonergan Workshop 1, edited by Fred Lawrence (Missouri, MT: Scholars
    Press, 1978), pp. 1-26.   It was originally a paper at the 1976
    Workshop.

11. Lonergan, Method, p. 40, with acknowledgment there of the work of
    Joseph de Finance as his source.

matter of successive stages of development, but dialectical, the
dismantling of the old and the establishment of the new, in the radical
transformation we call conversion.[12]

Now to effect such a radical change requires a great deal of
self-searching and even more a soul-struggle of epic proportions, which
is perhaps why Ignatius sets thirty days as the time to devote to his
Exercises. But the new analysis adds to the forces at work in the
change; it does not add them as new agents—they are provided by God and
were, presumably, as much at work in Abraham as in Ignatius—but it
makes us aware of them and so enables us to respond to them more effectively. The same dynamism that was exploited in Thomist analysis is, of
course, still operative: the dynamism of spirit open to the intelligible, to the true, to the good; a dynamism, let us always remember, that
is graced by God as well. But dialectic adds to our understanding by
invoking not only openness and response to the good but also the element
of personal encounter—a challenge not so clearly provided in a more
intellectualist context. This is a matter of "meeting persons, appre-
ciating the values they represent, criticizing their defects, and
allowing one's living to be challenged at its very roots by their words
and by their deeds."[13] That list, with the exception of the third item,
is verified par excellence in the encounter with Christ which we experience in the Ignatian Exercises.

Further, there is a remarkable parallel between dialectic as a
theological task and the structured process of the exercise on the Two
Standards. We bring to this exercise an assembly of materials from the
life of Christ, and complete the operations of experience, understanding, and judgment by adding that of evaluation (though these are
not four distinct tasks, as they are in theology). Again, there is a
structured path in methodical theology from dialectic through foundations to doctrines: "There are theological doctrines reached by the
application of a method that distinguishes functional specialties and
uses the functional specialty, foundations, to select doctrines from
among the multiple choices presented by the functional specialty, dia-

12. Lonergan, Method, pp. 106, 237, and passim; see the Index, under
    "Conversion," "Dialectic," "Horizon," etc.

13. Lonergan, Method, p. 247.

lectic."[14] This is closely paralleled in the Two Standards, if we take doctrines in the broad sense of judgments of fact and value, of human ways, of Christ's example, of God's guidance. For that exercise leads directly to the strange and unexpected and wholly unwelcome doctrine that Christ's way is exactly the opposite of our "natural" way that begins with love of wealth, leads on to desire for honor, and often ends in pride with its whole train of sin; the way of Christ begins with love of poverty, leads to desire for humble status, and so to humility and the whole range of virtues.[15]

There, put as briefly as possible, are my first two attempts to analyze the Exercises. As with Thomist ends and means, I still think Lonergan's dialectic is a valid and effective analytic tool and have seen no reason to abandon it. But I offered it eight years ago as a help toward understanding only the first half of the Exercises, leaving the Third and Fourth Weeks and the final Contemplation still outside the schema. At that time Lonergan had just begun to speak thematically of the two ways of human development, though they were implicit and all but thematic in Method's two phases of theology. Now, alerted by his reference, in every one of eight papers written from 1974 to 1977,[16] to this pair of movements in our development, I believe we can take a further step in the analysis of the Exercises. Here then is my third attempt.

The gist of my present view is that the analysis based on dialectic and effective for the First and Second Weeks, is notably complemented by considering the first half of the Exercises as basically an instance of the upward movement, and that what we need to add, for effective analysis of the second half, is the downward movement. I ask my readers to note the word, basically. I do not wish to be understood in a reductive and exclusive sense, as if the way of achievement, of acquisition by personal effort, were alone operative at first, and the other way, of receiving in love and trust, were alone operative later. It is a matter, rather, of the emphasis falling now on one and now on

---

14. Lonergan, Method, p. 298.

15. Spiritual Exercises, no. 146.

16. See note 4 to my preface, above.

the other, in such a way as to make one movement characteristic of the
first two weeks and the other characteristic of the last two. Perhaps
the word, focus, and an analogy with the levels of consciousness, will
be helpful: as research, while using all four levels, focuses on
experience and the assembly of data, so the first two weeks of the
Exercises, while consciously receiving and consciously relying on what
is received, nevertheless focuses on the acquisition of spiritual goods,
in a way that is not so evident in the last two weeks.

We can invoke another pair of Thomist terms here, and say that
the two phases of the Exercises (let us call them that, for simplicity's
sake) stand to one another as a bonum acquirendum does to a bonum communicandum, as a good to be acquired does to a good to be shared. In
the first we are concerned with what we may do, or achieve, or acquire,
and so the dynamism of ends and means remains fully operative. Nor
should this be interpreted as a selfish way: what we wish to acquire is,
or may be, extremely precious and noble—self-mastery and the conquest
of sin, the Christian virtues and even a place in the frontlines of
Christ's army, ultimately salvation. Still, it is something we strive
to acquire. It is an eros, but an eros in the sense in which Nygren
uses the term,[17] the sense in which the idea occurs over and over in the
scriptures themselves: "Store up treasure in heaven" (Mt 6:20); "I press
towards the goal to win the prize" (Phil 3:14).

The bonum communicandum is another story, offering possibilities
of another order altogether. This is not a good we reach out to grasp,
however laudably and meritoriously we might do so. It is rather a spontaneous overflow, a necessity that love has for sharing whatever we
possess with those we love and for entering into their state to share
with them what they experience or endure. Let me use again my favorite
example (with St. Thomas I prefer repeating the apt example to searching
my imagination for elegant variation). It is that of a mother who sits
with closed eyes by the cradle of her child. She does not open them
when she hears footsteps, to satisfy her curiosity of who is passing by.

---

17. Anders Nygren, Agape and Eros, translated by P. S. Watson (London:
    SPCK, 1953).—Notice that in unselfish acts the higher goals of eros
    overlap those of agape, and acquiring for ourselves overlaps
    acquiring for others, as when we become apostles for Christ. But
    the focus is still on achieving, and it is that focus which most
    radically distinguishes the first phase of the Exercises.

She does not look up in alarm when she hears brakes squealing down the
street. She remains as if sightless. Why? Because she is sharing the
state of her child who was born blind. What good is she doing by this
renunciation? What is she achieving or acquiring? What purpose does she
serve? The questions are all out of place; they belong in another context. The context now is the need love has to share with the one who is
loved, not the attraction of the "treasure," the "prize," the good one
may acquire.

Now this is very much our attitude in the second phase of the
Exercises. In the Third Week we share the sorrows and sufferings of
Christ, in the Fourth Week the peace and happiness he enjoys in the
resurrection. And from love's viewpoint (if viewpoint be not a misnomer
from the start) it does not matter, or at least is not a primary consideration, whether what we do results in some growth or gain, or
whether it is pleasant or unpleasant: what matters primarily is our
overarching, our overwhelming need to share with the one we love. In
this case, it is to be with Christ, wherever he may be: in suffering and
sorrow, if he happens to be in suffering and sorrow; in peace and happiness, if that is where he is. The end/means structure has given way to
a friendship/sharing one.[18]

Let me document more carefully my position on the two phases. In
the first phase of the Exercises the emphasis falls, therefore, on what,
with God's grace, I may achieve or acquire. This is true of the Principle and Foundation, which tells us to make ourselves indifferent to all
created things, for the sake of the supernal end. It is equally true of
the First Week's struggle to turn from sin, and even of its "for Christ"
motif: what have I done, what am I doing, what ought I to do for
Christ?[19] And it is true of the Second Week, with its petition, recur-

---

18. For the bonum communicandum and sharing in friendship as St. Thomas
    conceived them, one may consult such texts as these: Summa
    theologiae, I-II, q. 1, a. 4 ad 1m; q. 28, a. 4 ad 2m; q. 65, a. 5;
    II-II, q. 25, a. 3; q. 26, a. 2; III, q. 1, a. 1.—Note also that
    the Thomist judgment "by connaturality" corresponds to our movement
    from values to truth in development from above; see Summa
    theologiae, II-II, q. 45, a. 2, and passim in Thomas.

19. Spiritual Exercises, no. 53. The same motif is found, of course, in
    the Third Week (no. 197), but subordinate now to that of being with
    Christ. —I repeat here the admonition given in note 17, to the
    effect that acquiring for ourselves turns into acquiring for others

ring in all the exercises in which we contemplate the life of Christ,
for "an intimate knowledge of our Lord, who has become man for me, that
I may love Him more and follow Him more closely."[20]

That quotation points even more directly to what is characteristic of the first phase, the order, namely, of knowledge and love.
Aquinas regularly gives knowledge the priority in the sense that love
follows from knowledge, and the object of will is defined in terms of
the good that is understood and known.[21] The Thomist influence on
Lonergan was tenacious, so that even in Method, when all the elements
needed to establish the reverse order were at hand, he still tends to
think of the love which precedes judgment as an exception to what is
normal. This language continues in an early statement of the two ways
of development,[22] but in the two great lectures of 1977 has yielded to
what seems to me a more even presentation.[23] It would accord better, I
think, with his final position, to say that both ways are perfectly
normal, one normal to achievement, the other to reception; and, since we
are all our lives both receiving and achieving, the full normality is
the complementarity of the two.

With that in mind we may notice now how characteristic it is of
the first phase of the Exercises to put knowledge first and love second.
Thus the very Ignatian Triple Colloquy of the First Week asks for "knowledge of my sins and a feeling of abhorrence," for an understanding of
the disorder of my actions, with consequent horror, and for knowledge of

---

as we leave unselfishness behind. But we need more radical terms to
distinguish and relate the two main phases of the Exercises, and I
find them in the pair of ideas that have structured this whole book
and become applicable here as the complementary pair of achieving-
for and being-with.

20. Spiritual Exercises, no. 104.

21. The Thomist indices give numerous references for the statement:
    "Bonum intellectum est obiectum voluntatis," v.g., Summa
    theologiae, I, q. 21, a. 1 ad 2m; q. 82, a. 3 c. & ad 2m; a. 4; I-
    II, q. 13, a. 5 ad 2m; etc.

22. Lonergan, "Christology Today," A Third Collection, pp. 76-77.

23. Lonergan, "Natural Right and Historical Mindedness," A Third
    Collection, p. 181, and "Theology and Praxis," A Third Collection,
    pp. 196-197.

the world, again with consequent horror.[24] Horror is the negative counterpart of love here,[25] but the positive side is explicit in the already
quoted petition "for an intimate knowledge of our Lord ... that I may
love Him more." This becomes the pattern for the petitions of the
Second Week,[26] and returns in the changed Additions for that week:
directing myself on rising so as "to know better the eternal Word Incar-
nate in order to serve and follow Him more closely."[27] Thus, too, the
great pair of exercises on the Two Standards and the Three Pairs of Men
are related to one another as knowing the options in all their subtlety,
and choosing the right one in spite of my biases.[28] Finally, there is
the most characteristic feature of all, that the first phase leads up to
and culminates in the Election,[29] which is an act of will and therefore
of love in the broad sense.

It remains now to document more carefully my position on the
second phase of the Exercises. As it is characteristic, then, of the
first phase to seek the good, and indeed the highest good which is the
imitation of Christ as our way to God, so it is characteristic of the
second to be with Christ, to share with him in the communion of love, to
share in the same way with God in the final contemplation. Negatively,
the emphasis is no longer on a virtue to be gained, an amendment of
conduct to propose, a state of life to choose, a work to accomplish, an
achievement of any kind to be effected or any good to be acquired.
These remain as goals, but they are not the focus; the very notion
itself of goal becomes marginal. Positively, the stress is on the com-

---

24. Spiritual Exercises, no. 63.

25. Useful here: St. Thomas Aquinas, Summa theologiae, I-II, q. 26, de
amore, and q. 29, de odio.

26. Spiritual Exercises, nos. 104, 113, etc.

27. Spiritual Exercises, no. 130.

28. The first asks for knowledge of the ways of Satan and of Christ (no.
139) and the other for grace to choose what is more to God's glory
(no. 152).

29. The Second Week ends with instructions on the Election, nos. 169-
188, or (where the Ignatian election is not possible) on the reform
of life (no. 189).

munion, the sharing, the Mitsein, of love: sharing the suffering of
Christ in the Third Week and his joy in the Fourth, then sharing with
God our Creator in all that we have and are and do.[30]

Thus, in the petition of the first exercise of the Third Week, we
ask for sorrow, affliction, and confusion, because on account of my sins
the Lord is going to his Passion.[31]   There is effort to be expended,
there is great effort (magno nisu), but it is not directed to the reform
of life or the gaining of virtue: it is directed toward feeling what
Christ feels. The petition of the next exercise follows suit: we ask
for sorrow with Christ full of sorrows, we ask to be broken with Christ
broken, for tears and interior pain for the great pain which Christ
endured for us.[32] The Fourth Week has the same generic purpose, union
with Christ in his experience, only it is union with him now in his joy.
So the petition is for grace to rejoice and be glad, to rejoice and be
glad exceedingly, for the great glory and joy of Christ our Lord.[33] The
general lines of the contrast between first and second phase emerge more
clearly when we recall that throughout the Second Week the petition was
for knowledge in order that love might follow, and when we notice that
this sequence simply disappears from the Third and Fourth Weeks; we are
to act now as if we were in a state of love.

Those familiar with the Ignatian work will have been wondering at
my omission so far of any reference to the exercise called in some
translations, Three Degrees, in others, Three Modes, of Humility.[34]
They may suspect that I am in the position of a certain retreat-master
who told his audience, "I'm leaving this exercise out because I don't
understand it, and don't know what to do with it." I am not, of course,
omitting it: any analysis of the Exercises which failed to "explain"
this famous exercise would be self-condemned. I submit, however, that

---

30. Spiritual Exercises, nos. 203, 221, 231.

31. Spiritual Exercises, no. 193; the theme, with Christ, is clearer in
    no. 203.

32. Spiritual Exercises, no. 203. For the "magno nisu" phrase, see no.
    195.

33. Spiritual Exercises, no. 221.

34. Spiritual Exercises, no. 164.

it readily yields to analysis in our terms; it will, in fact, provide
illumination for the whole thrust of this Appendix. I will introduce my
study by affirming that chronologically, in the sequence of the various
exercises, it is located in the Second Week, but in idea and spirit it
belongs to the Third. To understand this, and why Ignatius located it
where he did, will furnish a key to the Exercises as a whole, and
especially to the transition from first phase to second.

First, then, the idea and spirit of the Three Modes or Degrees is
that of the Third Week. For the first two degrees are presented as
avoidance of all sin and all imperfection of any kind, so that for no
consideration whatever would the exercitant entertain for a moment the
slightest thought of the slightest sin; in effect, the aim is a life of
perfect virtue. Now the third degree purports to go further, but what
on earth could there be that goes beyond a life of perfect virtue?
Logic would say, Nothing whatever. Ignatius, however, discovers a positive answer. It is this: given the option of poverty or riches, of
opprobrium or honor, of a name for being useless and stupid or for being
wise and prudent in this world--to choose the first member in each case
rather than the second. Why make such a choice? There is no evil to
overcome, no good to accomplish, no purpose to serve, no virtue to
acquire, no service rendered to God; by hypothesis all these "ends" and
"goals" are achieved in the first two degrees, where all choices "would
promote equally the service of God our Lord and the salvation of my
soul."[35] The one reason—and it is not a reason except in the sense in
which Pascal said that the heart has reasons which reason does not know
—is the force that is operative in the Third and Fourth Weeks: this is
the way Christ went, and we follow, not in imitation of a virtue but in
the communion of love. We are not, then, choosing poverty as good; we
are choosing poverty with Christ poor, opprobrium with Christ dis-
honored, ridicule with Christ ridiculed. One might say, from this viewpoint, that the third degree does not really go beyond the first two,
any more than the downward movement of tradition goes beyond the upward
movement of achievement; it is simply a different mode, belonging in
another context—one might speak, rather, of two degrees in one mode,
and of a second mode which differs radically from both degrees of the
first.

---

35. Spiritual Exercises, no. 166.

Three questions occur, however, on this analysis. The first: why is this exercise located within the Second Week? It is because Ignatius wants it to precede the Election of a state of life,[36] and the Election should not be deferred to the Third Week. It is to precede the Election in order to promote such an election as would be made after the Third Week by one who is in love, or acts as if in love, with the crucified Christ. Thus, though love is self-justifying, and does not build on formulated grounds but only on reasons that reason does not know, still the reason (of the head) can accept such unreasoned love as ground and reason for the choices it must make in its own performances. But, secondly, why love of the crucified instead of the risen Christ? Ignatius does not say, but it is easy to supply an answer: it is surely that this choice is more suited to our short life on earth, whereas there will be eternity to share with Christ in glory, to choose joy with Christ rather than sorrow, and so on. And thirdly, why therefore does Ignatius not postpone the Election till the Third Week? The answer would seem to be simply that the Election is a task to perform, a work to do, and one of high import. To focus on such a decision would distract the exercitant from the proper attitude of the second phase: feeling and experiencing with Christ the Lord, and sharing with God his Father; as a task, therefore, it belongs rather to the Second Week, though it is not to be achieved without anticipation of the mood proper to the Third.

We come, finally, to the last exercise in the Ignatian volume: the Contemplation to Gain Love. It is essentially one in idea and spirit with the generic attitude of the Third and Fourth Weeks, only now the loved one is God our Creator in the divinity that belongs to God as God. The spirit of the exercise appears in a preliminary remark of Ignatius: "love consists in a mutual sharing of goods."[37] But the scope is widened to a contemplation of all that God has given me, in Christ and the benefits of creation, in the divine presence to me, in the divine work and labor on earth, etc. And the corresponding response is not now the following of Christ, not as such, but our side of the "mutual sharing": hence a total oblation, which I make "as one would do

36. Spiritual Exercises, no. 164.

37. Spiritual Exercises, no. 231.

who is moved by great feeling," an oblation of liberty, memory, understanding, will, "all that I have and possess."[38] We noticed earlier
that the order of the Second Week, where love followed on knowledge, disappeared from the Third and Fourth.   It returns now, but with a difference; the emphasis is not on knowledge of a way to follow, but on
knowledge of blessings received, "that filled with gratitude for all, I
may in all things love and serve the Divine Majesty."[39]   It may be that
Ignatius, in this final exercise, is interweaving more closely the two
threads that had been given prominence one by one in earlier exercises.

That last sentence recalls a qualification I made in the beginning: to use the analytic tools of an upward and downward movement of
development in order to interpret the two phases of the Exercises is not
to say that either phase is explained reductively and exclusively by
just one of the movements.   To exaggerate the case here would be to ruin
it.   I wish, then, to conclude my documentary work by calling attention
to the presence of both strands throughout the Ignatian set of exercises.   Thus, the first phase is not simply the upward way from
experience through understanding and judgment to consequent decision.
On the contrary the way of love is made operative very early: in the
contemplation of Christ on the cross and of what he has done for me,[40]
in the wondering exclamation that God has not annihilated me,[41] in
thanksgiving and affection toward God who has kept me from eternal
punishment.[42]   Similarly, the second phase is not simply the downward
way of loving reception of God's gift: there is stern effort, the magno
nisu of the Third Week,[43] there is fruitful application to be made—the
fructum capere of both Third and Fourth Weeks,[44] there is the very title

---

38. Spiritual Exercises, no. 234.

39. Spiritual Exercises, no. 233.

40. Spiritual Exercises, no. 53.

41. Spiritual Exercises, no. 60.

42. Spiritual Exercises, no. 71.

43. Spiritual Exercises, no. 195.

44. Spiritual Exercises, nos. 194 (where the phrase occurs three times)
and 222 (which refers back to no. 194).

of the last exercise which is a contemplation to gain love, and there
are the general procedures of prayer throughout the book—determining a
topic, forming a picture, proposing a need to be the object of my
petition, all of them more characteristic of effort toward a hoped for
achievement.[45]   This is brightly illuminated by the community-in-
contrast of a pair of oblations made in the Exercises. There is the
oblation made in the Kingdom exercise, which introduces the Second Week
and consists in offering myself for the work: I will follow Christ and
labor with him for the great purpose.[46]   And there is the oblation of
the last exercise in the volume, which is an offering of what I have and
am.[47]   There is a similar community-in-contrast when we turn to the two
ways of imitating Christ: such imitation is thematic in the Second Week,
but it is that of the disciple learning true virtue from a master; now
the idea occurs also in the Three Modes of Humility,[48] but here the
imitation is more that of a lover sharing the state of the beloved. A
brief but not inaccurate summary would seem to be that the first phase
has achievement as a focus, with love as supplement, while the second
has love as a focus, with achievement as supplementary.

    One can hardly enter into the Ignatian Exercises, or ponder their
dynamism, without a sharper realization of the need and power of images
in human consciousness. Let our concluding reflections, then, return to
our early effort to find an appropriate image for the two ways of human
development. The original image of upward and downward movements served
the useful purpose of distinguishing the two, and allowed us to relate
the four conscious operations of each within a single dynamism; but it
did not provide equally well for the unity of the two movements: they
seem merely to cancel one another out. The image of two vectors which
we exploited in chapter one is still useful for ordinary education, but

---

45. The Ignatian pattern is to state the topic and, after a preparatory
    prayer, to make the First Prelude, which is "a mental representation
    of the place" (no. 47), and the Second Prelude, in which I "ask God
    our Lord for what I want and desire" (no. 48). He adds: "The
    Preparatory Prayer ... and the two Preludes ... must always be made
    before all contemplations and meditations" (no. 49).

46. Spiritual Exercises, nos. 95, 97.

47. Spiritual Exercises, no. 234: "all I possess and myself with it."

48. Spiritual Exercises, no. 167.

it introduces a measure of tension (the two forces tend only partially in the same direction) and does not seem wholly appropriate for educa- tion in the schola Christi. One could think of two streams uniting to flow together to a common goal, but the characteristic differences are not brought out then. The best image that occurs to me is the unlikely one of an airplane carried forward by a combination of propeller and jet, the propeller pulling on the air in front (like the arms pulling on the rung of a ladder) and the jet pushing on the wall of the air behind (like the feet pushing on the rung below). Readers may easily find flaws in the comparison, or even argue which airplane engine corresponds to which way of human development, but it may help us conceive in some imperfect fashion the two ways we are carried forward, driven by a built-in dynamism that heads for the true and the good, but also

by the love impelled

That moves the sun in heaven and all the stars.[49]

The love that moves, not only the sun in heaven and all the stars but also the minds and hearts of men and women and children, is divine grace and so mystery. When we have done all that analysis can do, let us remember that our thinking, even at the very best of an Aquinas, is only straw, to be devoured finally in the flame of mystery understood.

---

49. The concluding words of Dante's Divina Commedia, as translated by H. F. Cary.